Also by Bruce Larson

Living Beyond Our Fears

The Presence

A Call to Holy Living

Faith for the Journey

My Creator, My Friend

Wind and Fire

Communicator's Commentary: Luke

Believe and Belong

There's a Lot More to Health Than Not Being Sick

Dare to Live Now

Living on the Growing Edge

No Longer Strangers

The One and Only You

Thirty Days to a New You

Risky Christianity

The Meaning and Mystery of Being Human

Setting Men Free

The Emerging Church

Ask Me to Dance

With J. Keith Miller:

The Edge of Adventure

Living the Adventure

The Passionate People: Carriers of the Spirit

What God Wants to Know

Finding Your Answers in God's Vital Questions

BRUCE LARSON

HarperSanFrancisco
A Division of HarperCollins*Publishers*

WHAT GOD WANTS TO KNOW: *Finding Your Answers in God's Vital
Questions.* Copyright © 1993 by Bruce Larson. All rights reserved.
Printed in the United States of America. No part of this book may
be used or reproduced in any manner whatsoever without written
permission except in the case of brief quotations embodied in criti-
cal articles and reviews. For information address HarperCollins
Publishers, 10 East 53rd Street, New York, NY 10022.

FIRST EDITION

Library of Congress Cataloging-in-Publication Data
Larson, Bruce.
    What God wants to know: finding your answers in God's vital
questions / Bruce Larson.
        p.   cm.
    ISBN 0-06-065012-5 (alk. paper)
    1. Spiritual life—Christianity.   2. Dialogue—Religious as-
pects—Christianity.   3. Listening—Religious aspects—Christianity.   4. Prayer—Christianity.   I. Title.
BV4501.2.L3323 1993
248.4—dc20   92-56107
                                                                                              CIP

93 94 95 96 97 ❖ HAD 10 9 8 7 6 5 4 3 2 1

This edition is printed on acid-free paper that meets the
American National Standards Institute Z39.48 Standard.

To Mallory, Hannah, and Abigail,
Children of my children
and children of God

Contents

Foreword

I HAVE BEEN WAITING for a book like this for a long time. I congratulate Bruce Larson, my friend for over thirty years and more recently my co-pastor at the Crystal Cathedral, for writing a book about prayer as dialogue with God.

For years I have been encouraging people to listen to God and act on their dreams. When we listen God can give us His new ideas for change. Prayer should be as much listening to God as it is telling Him of our needs.

Larson plunges us into the Bible as our basic text for discovering the miracle of dialogue with God. The questions God asks us reveal His unconditional love for us and help us discern how we are to live so that He can bless us and make us significant people to our contemporaries.

Reading *What God Wants to Know* will make your heart sing. You will discover in new ways how much God loves you and what a great future He has for you if you listen and obey.

Robert H. Schuller

Preface

A WORD OF WARNING to anyone who is about to read this book: this is a book about God, not a book about theology. Mostly, I find theology unexciting. I think that seminaries and divinity schools in general focus far too much on theology.

Theology literally means "the science of God." But God is not a science that requires study. Rather, He is the author of science—and of everything else that exists.

God may be no more interested in theology than I am in Bruceology—the science of Bruce. He has revealed Himself throughout the Bible and in the history of human events as a Creator who wants to have a relationship with the men and women whom He has created. He may not want to be studied. He may, rather, want to love and be loved.

The single most important question for any of us is, "Is there a God?" Having created us in His own image, He has given us free will, and we must exercise that free will in either accepting or rejecting Him. He cannot make us love Him or even believe in Him. And as we move into a relationship with Him, He presents us with particular challenges and a number of pointed questions.

These questions are ones that God has asked His people throughout the Bible. They provide a clearer picture of who He is—His nature, His love, and His purposes. Our answers to those questions today are an indication of where we are in our journey of faith, and in a real way we are judged by our responses.

It is with this premise in mind that this book has been written. The knowledge we have about God through both Old and New Testaments indicates that He loves us, that He wants to know us, and that He wants us to know Him. The questions He asks all through the biblical narrative can provide the vehicle for that deepening relationship.

Even those of us who have been solidly in the Christian camp for many years are sometimes puzzled over two issues. First, who exactly is God and what is His nature? Second, what does He want of us, His children? This book is an attempt to deal with those two issues from an unusual perspective—by examining ten questions that God has been asking us over the centuries. As we do so, my hope is that you, the reader, along with me, will gain fresh insight into what it means to enter into dialogue with our Creator, our Redeemer, and our Friend.

Acknowledgments

I HAVE WRITTEN over twenty books, but this one is different. God gave me the complete outline while I was recovering from cancer surgery in a hospital. It was my first stay in a hospital and the first time I outlined a book in just five days. My previous books were years in the making.

With the outline in mind I took some study leave and checked into a hotel for two weeks and wrote the first rough draft. God was surely in it, for it seemed to flow effortlessly. But the result is not this book.

My wife, Hazel, took my draft and spent months editing, reorganizing, rewriting, and adding illustrations. The book is as much hers as mine—a genuine three-way partnership with the Holy Spirit.

I'm grateful to my friends at Harper San Francisco for believing in this book and for the creative editorial help graciously given by Beth Weber.

Finally, I want to thank Sharleen LaJeunesse for tireless typing and constant encouragement.

Introduction:
The Turning Point

"LORD, LET ME LIVE long enough to be a problem to my children," reads the message on my friend's refrigerator. It is a sentiment that can be appreciated by anyone who has had teenaged children.

My wife and I had our share of problems with all three of our teenagers, but none more acute than those with our middle child, Peter. At one point, communication had broken down to such an extent that, in the interest of peace and sanity, we seriously considered sending him off to a distant private school which we could ill afford.

The more we corrected Peter and told him what he should do and be, the more aloof, withdrawn, and superior he seemed to become. Then one day, when I was working at home and went to his room for some typing paper, I discovered a poem he had written that totally changed my perception of him.

> Hello out there, world;
> It's me in here . . .
> Who am I? You say I don't sound like myself?
> That's because you've never heard me.

This other guy? Oh, he's the shell I told you about.
You say that's me?
No, I'm in here;
He's just my protection.

I was devastated by his poem. It sparked the beginning of genuine communication between Peter and me as I started to really listen to the unhappy boy inside that shell.

Listening is hard work. Ask any psychologist or psychiatrist, physician or pastor, or anyone who makes a living at listening. It is so much easier to give advice or suggest solutions.

Last year during a short holiday in England, my wife and I were riding on a train from London up to the Lake District. In the two seats across the aisle sat two senior women. From the moment they got on the train neither one stopped speaking. They rode along for about an hour and a half, both talking the entire time. I'm sure they were the best of friends, but I wonder how much they could ever really learn about each other—neither was able to listen.

We remain mysteries until we choose to reveal ourselves to someone else. When we do, we need that other person to listen and try to interpret our words.

I have spent many years of my life doing workshops in churches across our country and around the world. I will often ask participants, "What was your first experience of unconditional love and what did that other person do to make you feel that way?" Among the thousands of responses to that question, I hear most frequently, "It was when he or she really listened to me." Someone has said that aggressive and intense listening appears and feels exactly like love.

It is natural to want and need someone to love us. That includes listening to us. Listening is the basis for any loving relationship. Have you ever thought about what God wants to say to you in those quiet moments when you are communicating with Him? Even God must want us to listen to Him, to hear what He is saying, and to understand His heart.

Typically, we approach Christianity with a list of questions and concerns. Before we will believe, we want some answers: What about the people who have never heard the Good News? What about the unfairness of life? Why do bad things happen to good people? Why weren't my prayers answered? Why wasn't my child healed? These are all valid questions, but perhaps we are approaching faith from the wrong direction. Perhaps we need to stop asking questions of God and start listening to the questions God asks us.

Discovering that my son Peter had something to say to me marked a turning point in our relationship. In the same way, discovering that God has questions for us marks a turning point in our relationship with Him.

We may bring our concerns to Him, of course, but in our dialogue He has particular questions for us. Some of His questions are personal, about our relationships, habits, ethics, or future plans, but others are more generic (in the sense that they have been asked by Him throughout the biblical narrative).

The notion that God has questions for us transformed the prayer life of one of my heroes and mentors, Paul Tournier, a physician whose writings on the inner life of the Christian are among the finest that I have read.

Paul Tournier was born in Geneva, Switzerland. His father was a Presbyterian pastor who died when Paul was less than two years old; his mother died shortly thereafter. Paul was raised by an uncle who was killed some years later in a car driven by Paul Tournier. In spite of, or perhaps because of, these multiple tragedies, Paul became a devout Christian. He believed in God and the Apostles' Creed, and he regularly read his Bible and went to church. Then something new came into his life, a change which he described in the foreword to my book, *Setting Men Free.*

"I recall that most decisive period in my life, well over thirty years ago, when I suddenly discovered in a personal way those utterly simple yet fundamental and living truths which the reader will find in this book.

"To be sure, I was then already a Christian, and had been very active in church endeavors.

"The mere exhortation that I move from theory to practice would not have been effectual for me at that time. It took an inner movement to bring this about, a prodding which is born of precisely one thing: personal dialogue.... I ... took the steps to where I could hear God, could discover freedom, solidarity, the personal encounter with Jesus Christ and my neighbor, and could come to know the art of living."

Paul kept a regular quiet time each morning with his wife, Nellie. They would wake early, go to separate rooms, read their Bibles, and talk to God.

One day Tournier heard an inner voice say to him, "Paul, why is it you are always asking me questions? Why don't you start listening to me and begin to let me ask you some questions?"

Tournier was stunned. But he understood that the message was from God; from that moment he began to listen as well as talk during his prayer time. He kept a journal in which he recorded those questions that God seemed to be asking him. The questions were varied: "Paul, why were you so short-tempered with Nellie at dinner last night?"; "Paul, why are you afraid to confront that patient you saw yesterday and tell her the truth?"; "Paul, why did you make that extravagant purchase last week?"

This practice of personal dialogue marked a turning point for Paul Tournier. It didn't just change his relationship to God, it prompted him to begin a new kind of dialogue with people. He started to listen aggressively to his wife, his patients, and his colleagues, and he was free to be vulnerable with them. This new kind of dialogue resulted in a more meaningful, loving relationship with God and with his fellow human beings.

Isn't it credible that God yearns to be heard by us as much as we yearn and ache to be heard by Him? There could be a loneliness even in the heart of God for genuine dialogue.

A remarkable three-way dialogue was a regular part of worship for the early Christians. The church was at its most powerful in those first three hundred years when a handful of laymen took on the Roman empire and transformed it. During those years confession took place in the homes of worshiping Christians. Before they worshiped they would confess their sins to

God before one another. In that climate of worship, in the presence of God, believers shared their lives.

By the end of the first three hundred years, the church had grown to the extent that clergy were needed, and professionals entered the scene. The church decided that confession could only take place one-on-one with a priest or in the midst of a worshiping congregation. From the year 600 to the time of the Reformation, confession was limited entirely to dialogue with a priest. The Reformation, which should have reopened dialogue between God and believers, closed it entirely. The reformers believed one's sins could only be forgiven by the High Priest in heaven; confession was abolished. Meaningful dialogue about real problems and sins was no longer an integral part of the community of believers. We Protestants became very closed people. It has been suggested that the pervasiveness of mental illness can be traced to that very time.

It is a turning point for all of us when we reopen this meaningful dialogue with God. In that context, He guides us by pointing out ways we can serve Him and change the lives of the people around us. But don't just settle for His guidance. Start that two-way relationship. Listen to God and hear those eternal questions that began in the Garden of Eden and continue to motivate and shape us today. As you respond to them, you may find yourself in a whole new dimension of discipleship.

WHAT GOD WANTS TO KNOW

CHAPTER ONE

"Where Are You?"

MY WIFE WAS teaching a women's Bible class some years back, and the topic was the creation story. As she began, she asked if there weren't some things her students might wish God had done differently in terms of His creation. There were a number of inventive suggestions: "He should have made us all the same color"; "A temperate climate in all parts of the world would be an improvement." But the room erupted in laughter when an elderly woman raised her hand and said forcefully, "I just wish He had given us some other method of procreation!"

The creation story as we find it in the beginning of the Old Testament has been the subject of considerable controversy over the years. Some aspects of it may seem implausible. Was all that we see created in seven days? Did the human race evolve from just one man and one woman?

One theory advanced is that time as we measure it is not necessarily God's time and seven days could be an indeterminate number of years. Further, Adam and Eve may be representative of the earliest race of people and not just two people. But however we understand the details, the Genesis record is clear: God is the Creator, and at some point He breathed His

Spirit into a race of people created in His own image, different from the animals, who possessed free will and a sense of right and wrong.

God's intent in bringing those first people into being was that He might have a relationship of love with them. We read in the book of Genesis that God walked with Adam and Eve in the cool of the day. There must have been much dialogue during those daily walks in the Garden. We can imagine the questions Adam and Eve had for God and the occasional question He had for them. The very first recorded question was asked just after the Fall, which is the term used for the event that precipitated the expulsion from Paradise and the subsequent alienation from God.

Our first ancestors broke the one and only commandment they had been given, and they became ashamed of their nakedness. They hid from each other behind fig leaves, and they hid from God behind the bushes. In that first question, God asked Adam, "Where are you?"

That question, so simple and direct, had and continues to have enormous implications. We could say it is perhaps the first question that God asks of anyone when He gets his or her attention. Adam and Eve broke a clear and simple commandment. That first question, in the wake of their rebellion, reveals so much about the nature of our Creator. But let's look first at the questions He did *not* ask. They are just as revealing.

For example, He did not say, like Santa Claus, "Have you been a good little boy? Have you been a good little girl?" He is omniscient. He knew that they had not been good just as He knows that we have not been good. Part of the Good News of the Bible is that we are all bad: "All have sinned and fall short of the glory of God." That is a given.

God's first question was not, "Why have you done this?" Psychologists, psychoanalysts, and psychotherapists of today are fascinated with that question. But after a lifetime of pursuing the whys of human behavior, I have concluded that insight alone is not very liberating. Even after years of analysis or counseling, we are often still groping toward self-understanding. But even if I do understand my own actions or yours and the deep motives and causes behind them, that knowledge does not free me from defeating behavior or crippling attitudes.

Alcoholics Anonymous, that amazing movement that has helped thousands of men and women find sobriety in this century, was founded by two men, Bill Wilson and Dr. Bob. Through the power of God in a small Episcopal church in New York City, these two overcame their own addictions and consequently devised a program to help others find help. Their initial program was unsuccessful, and they asked their rector, Sam Shoemaker, for advice. What was wrong? Why wasn't it working? He asked them if this was the program that had helped them. It wasn't. It was based on information they had read in psychology books.

They scrapped that first program and replaced it with the existing Twelve-Step program, which follows exactly their own route to recovery. The Twelve-Step program does not begin with the question of why. It begins with the admission that one is powerless over an addiction and moves on to acknowledging the existence of a Higher Power and to making a commitment to that Higher Power. Those first three steps can be applied effectively to all sorts of problems. Searching for the *why*, on the other hand, can prove unproductive and unending.

A third question God did not ask is, "What can I do?" He did not move in to fix everything. Adam and Eve erected a terrible barrier between themselves and God by their disobedience. How could that be reconciled and the Utopia that existed before the fall be restored?

God was not entirely surprised by this new state of affairs. He created people with free will. If I as a parent can predict fairly accurately what my children will do and say in certain circumstances, God understands His creation far more completely. He must have known all along that there would be a terrible price to pay at the heart of His creation if He was to continue in a relationship with His people.

So the cross was not an afterthought. Our omniscient God knows the beginning and the end. He had a plan and knew how that plan would unfold. He revealed that plan in bits and pieces all through the Old Testament, especially through prophets such as Isaiah and Jeremiah. They give us vivid glimpses into what would be required for God to once again be in relationship with His people as our Friend and Creator and Redeemer.

Finally, God did not say, "How dare you?" and separate Himself from Adam and Eve, though that would seem logical. They were tainted, and He is a perfect creator, and He cannot tolerate sin. The conviction that man is sinful while God is perfect is the premise of all religion. If He is not perfect, He is not God. How, then, can we earn our way into His presence? Will enough prayer or giving or devotion or sacrifice do it? It has always struck me that, in the Genesis story, it was man who moved away from the original comfortable relationship with God. God did not withdraw like some easily shocked maiden aunt. He was back in the same place at the same time looking to continue the relationship.

Those are some of the things God did *not* ask in that original dialogue, but what do we learn from the simple question that He *did* ask: "Where are you?"

The question indicates, first of all, that God is our friend. He has not withdrawn from us. He still wants to have a relationship with us. He still loves us. In that same book of the Bible, Abraham is called a friend of God. We read that "Abraham trusted God and it was counted to him as righteousness and he was called a friend of God." That is a radically different definition of *righteousness* than most religious people would understand or accept. While we equate righteousness with sinlessness or good works, God seems to settle simply for our trust.

God's question also indicates that God knows the worst. He knows the evil that's been done, and He still loves us. He is not shocked, but He is grieved. It's useless to hide. We cannot keep any secrets from Him.

That simple question also reveals God's forgiving nature. Whatever Adam and Eve have done, God expects the relationship to continue. He does not storm off in anger; rather, He is in the same place at the same time, making reconciliation possible.

God's first question is a difficult one for all of us. He still wants to know "Where are you? Why are you hiding from me?"

In spite of those fig leaves and trees, He sees us and calls to us to come out from our hiding places and trust Him.

Fearful as he was, Adam answered that first question. He told God he was ashamed of what he had done. Unfortunately, he went on to offer a self-defense. He denied that he had any part in this and pretended to be innocent. He blamed Eve, who in turn blamed the serpent. In fact, he even implicated God. He told God that "*this* woman [he refers to her impersonally, not as "my wife" or "Eve" but as *this* woman] whom *you* gave me, gave me the forbidden fruit." In other words, "It is not my fault. As a matter of fact, God, it is partly Your fault. You gave me the wrong partner, and she tempted me to sin."

Incidentally, for most of the early church fathers, Eve was the real villain in the Garden of Eden story, and she and her sex have suffered considerable discrimination and oppression as a result. Tertullian, who's been called the first great genius among Christian writers, after the apostles, wrote in *De culte terminarum:* "Do you not know that you are each an Eve? The sentence of God on this sex of yours lives in this age. . . . You are the devil's gateway . . . the first deserter of the divine law. . . ."

Just recently Hebrew scholars have discovered that the translation of the word describing Eve as "helpmate" is in error. That word, *ezer-kenegdo*, means "equal to him" or "corresponding to him." God did not make any second-class human beings. Eve was created equal to and exactly like Adam and was not any more guilty than he.

"Where are you?" Like Adam, we are still answering that first question with all sorts of defenses. We say we are in trouble but it isn't our fault. We are the product of a dysfunctional family. We have children who disappoint us after all we've done for them. We have a spouse who does not love us enough or in the right way. We did not get enough education. We are the wrong color, we aren't good-looking, our health is poor, we were born in the wrong part of the world. Much of this has to be God's fault since He made us. We, like Adam, resort to blaming God for our problems.

Jim McCord, the former president of Princeton Theological Seminary, was my friend and mentor. Among the many lessons he taught me and others is this one: "To sin is man's condition. To pretend that he's not a sinner, that is man's sin." Our separation from God is the result of our pretended innocence, not our guilt. God can deal with our guilt, but our self-justification keeps Him at arm's length, and the arm is ours.

A common defense we use when God is seeking us out is that everybody is doing it. This is the answer looters gave in the 1992 Los Angeles riots. They were stealing all sorts of things, even things for which they had no use. Childless people were hauling off boxes of disposable diapers, and nonsmokers were grabbing cartons of cigarettes. Caught in the act by reporters, they always gave the same explanation: "Everybody's doing it." The rationale here is, if everybody sins, nobody sins. That way nobody is accountable.

As God pursues us, as He did Adam, we sometimes respond with another kind of defense. We say, "I'm not so bad. I'm probably better than most people." Many of us have a hard time coming to grips with the fact that we've ever done anything wrong. We take comfort in being better than our neighbor. We don't drink as much, we don't mess around, we work hard, we're devoted to our family. What does sin have to do with us and our lives? Sin is what we read about in the papers every day—murders, armed robberies, arson, kidnapping. It is a major turning point for any of us to come to the realization that whatever our behavior, good or bad, we are selfish people and that were it not for God's presence and grace, we would act entirely out of our own self-interest. Further, sin, in essence, is more than particular unlovely acts; it is whatever separates us from God, including our pride and our self-righteousness.

Our response to God's question, "Where are you?" might be provisional. "Sometime in the future I *will* come out of hiding and meet you, God, but first I want to have some fun." We do not believe that God wants to give us joy and fulfillment. We believe Jesus came to make us good in some frightfully boring way. We want to live life to the full before we start being God's person. Even St. Augustine is said to have prayed, "Oh, God, make me pure, but not yet." We see God as some cosmic killjoy, rather than the author of all that is truly exciting and satisfying.

I'm sure that, like me, you've heard people say, "I'm afraid that if I meet God and give Him my life He will send me out as a missionary in some remote jungle." Realistically, why would God send anyone to a place he or she does not want to go to bring Good News about His grace and His love? The assumption is that God is determined to make us do difficult and unpleasant things for which we have no passion or inclination.

Some of us ignore God's question about where we are because we feel we don't need God. We think we are perfectly happy without God. Why should we respond to Him? But that posture—that we are happy and self-sufficient and our lives are together—takes a lot of psychic energy to maintain.

When I was living in Maryland, I bought a little Honda motorcycle to commute between my home and my office. It was scary to drive down six-lane highways on that tiny machine, but at the same time it was exciting to whiz along, dressed in my business suit, with my briefcase strapped behind me and my helmet clapped on my head. The airstream from all the other vehicles almost blew me off the road.

One morning I managed to run right into a wasp. It flew inside my shirt and began to sting me repeatedly. I didn't dare pull off the road immediately as I didn't want to alarm the other drivers. Instead, I tried to look calm and composed till I could find a place to stop and park with safety. I whipped off my shirt and killed the wasp, but it had already done a lot of damage, and I counted any number of bites.

That experience gave me a fresh insight into the human condition. People all around us are being bitten by the wasp of meaninglessness and purposelessness and powerlessness. What an effort it takes to keep looking pleasant and unruffled in order to keep up a front for the world. James Lynch, a medical researcher at Johns Hopkins Hospital, is convinced that loneliness is the number-one killer in America. In his book *The Broken Heart* he claims that loneliness is the primary factor in deaths due to heart attacks and cancer. We can look self-sufficient and happy, though all the while we are being stung to death by loneliness. A country-and-western song I've heard recently makes the claim that loneliness is the nearest thing to death. According to James Lynch, loneliness is the vestibule to death.

Perhaps we are hiding and won't answer God's question because we are convinced we are beyond hope. We think that even God's grace cannot help us. We have messed up so often and for so long that we cannot be redeemed. The Bible speaks of an unforgivable sin: the refusal to admit that we are guilty or to believe that we can be forgiven. Every other sin is forgivable.

Bernie Segal, a cancer surgeon, in his book *Peace, Love and Healing*, tells of making rounds in a ward where people are dying. When he asks a patient, "How are you?" the response often is, "You know how I am. I'm dying." "I know that," counters Segal, "but in the meantime what are you doing?" Invariably, the patient smiles and says, "I'm living." So long as we are alive, we are not spiritually dead, whatever our past, since God has revealed His grace and love and mercy to us so abundantly.

Then there are those who refuse to come out of hiding because they insist on justice rather than mercy. Sinners ought to rot in hell. Deathbed conversions shouldn't count. Evildoers deserve God's wrath and punishment. We want justice, and in a sense we all want to be judged. We know that cheap grace is worthless.

There's a story I read years ago about a man who died and went to some purgatorylike place, a staging area where you are sorted out for heaven or hell. In the distance are two doors—one clearly marked Heaven and the other clearly marked Hell. An official at the desk speaks to the new arrival: "We're terribly busy today; there's no time for you to be judged. Just choose a door. You can take either one." The man protests, "Wait a minute. I demand judgment. I want to know which door I deserve." "I'm sorry," explains the official, "we're seriously backlogged, and we haven't time to judge you. Just choose whichever door you want and move on quickly. We have others waiting." In despair the man shrugs, looks at both doors, and walks through the one marked Hell.

It's an intriguing story, and I'm convinced it's possible that some people do not want heaven. They want what they deserve.

Another answer to "Where are you?" is that we are going to stay hidden in our bushes until God answers some serious questions for us. We have intellectual doubts. What about the virgin birth? How are we supposed to believe in Jesus' Resurrection? Why do good people suffer? What will happen to those who have never heard the Good News? But we can come into the kingdom at the simplest level and trust God to reveal more of His nature and His will as our relationship with Him deepens.

As God asks His simple question we are forced to look around at those places where we are hiding. In Adam's case, it was the bushes. A lot of us are hiding in simple busyness. C. S. Lewis, in his wonderful book *The Great Divorce*, paints an unusual picture of heaven and hell. Those in hell are free to take a bus to heaven. It runs every day, and many of hell's residents make that trip. They are met at the gates by friends from their earthly life who escort them in. There are no walls around heaven, and anyone can stay, but few of the bus passengers choose to do so. One man was a bishop on earth, and his reason for not staying is that he is preparing a theological paper to be delivered to a group in hell. He is too busy to stay in the Celestial City. Our busyness can be a barrier between God and us even when we are busy with good and noble causes—church work, teaching, volunteerism. Then there's the humdrum busyness of everyday jobs, family, financial concerns.

Our hiding places are as varied as our personalities. We may be hiding in some addiction—to drugs, alcohol, illicit sex, overeating, or any other kind of compulsive behavior. More than one person has said to me, "I wish I were an alcoholic. It would be so nice to put a label on my problem, to go to AA and get help and find God."

The Bible tells us to trust God and to love people. But that advice has gotten twisted into something slightly different. We have changed the injunction into "love God and trust people." Trusting people is the certain path to disappointment. Most people are like you and me; they are not trustworthy. I may betray you. I may gossip about you. I may promise to pray for you and forget to do so. But I need and want your love in spite of my shortcomings. God is the only one who is trustworthy. We can come out of hiding and trust Him with our lives and our future and even our sins, past, present, and future.

I came out of my hiding place for the first time many years ago while I was still in seminary. I spent a long evening in a fellow student's room and told him who I was—all the dark and shadowy parts as well as the good. After we prayed I felt a great sense of liberation. Because I trusted God I could come out of hiding and begin to love my brothers and sisters.

If there is such a thing as a right answer to this first question God put to the first man, it must be to admit that we do hide from God. He knows that, and that's why He asks the question. Hiding places are not always unwholesome activities. Sometimes they are positive things that simply preoccupy our thoughts and take up too much of our time. Here's a test. Let's say you are sitting in church and feeling slightly bored. Where does your mind go to relieve that boredom? What do you find yourself thinking about? What is it you can't wait to get to or begin to do? That may very well be your hiding place.

God is pursuing all of us in those hiding places. He wants us to come out and walk with Him, not just in the cool of the day, but all day, every day.

CHAPTER TWO

"Where Is Your Brother?"

SOME YEARS AGO, on a Sunday afternoon in the dead of winter, my wife, Hazel, and I drove to New York from our New Jersey home through a snowstorm to attend a special event. Paul Tournier, whom I mentioned earlier, was to speak at Fifth Avenue Presbyterian Church, his first American appearance. We had read his books and were really excited about hearing him in person.

He spoke no English, but he had a very able translator, and his opening sentence grabbed our attention right off. He said, "Every Christian needs two conversions: one out of the world and one back into it." He stressed the need to move beyond personal piety to a concern for our brothers and sisters all over the globe. His text for that message might very well have been the second question of God's—to Cain, brother of Abel and son of Adam and Eve: "Where is your brother?"

We have just the bare bones of the story, famous as it is, and we don't know what really happened. We do know that Cain was enraged because he felt that God preferred his brother, Abel, and was more pleased with the sacrifice that Abel had offered to Him. Whether the offense was real or imagined, Cain, in a jealous rage, killed his brother. It is history's first recorded murder.

Did God love Abel more than Cain? Or did Cain just imagine that? A lot of us have been led down the wrong track because we imagined something to be true when it was not and acted on our perceptions as though they were fact. But it is possible that Cain read the situation rightly.

Does God have favorites? Think for a moment about two people sitting side by side in the same church, worshiping each Sunday. One is there simply out of love for God, thankful for His love and friendship and for the gift of life and relationship. This is someone who could say with Job, "Even if you slay me I will trust you." The second worshiper keeps reminding God of how faithful and good and sacrificial he has always been and how it's about time he was rewarded; God owes him something. Both people attend the church regularly, both are tithers or more, but they have totally different attitudes. It's not hard to believe that God is more pleased with the one who returns His unconditional love with unconditional love. Wouldn't you be?

Whether God preferred Abel to Cain or not, He was not put off by Cain's actions. He appeared at the scene. He is still the loving God and Creator, even when one of His children has committed the gravest of crimes. His question to Cain seems restrained in light of what had happened: "Where is your brother?" Being God, He already knew where Cain's brother was, and further, He knew what Cain had done.

But the question gave Cain a chance to own his guilt and acknowledge what he had done. Think of how the course of human events might have been altered had Cain simply answered God honestly: "Well, Sir, I perceived that you liked Abel better, and I couldn't stand it, and so I killed him in a fit of anger. I was wrong! I am sorry. Please forgive me. How can I make restitution?" Such an answer could have changed the whole of biblical history. Cain had a chance to model for us how to respond to God when we have been at our worst.

But what did he say? His answer was flippant, even rude: "How should I know? Am I my brother's keeper?" The Hebrew word used here for *keeper* is used only in connection with animals. Cain's retort translates into, "Am I the shepherd of my brother? Am I to be responsible for what happens to him?" Cain's answer was similar to the one his parents gave when confronted by their sins. He implied that he was not only innocent but ignorant of any wrongdoing.

We could interpret God's question to Cain as an invitation to test His grace and forgiveness even for the sin of murder. Cain's defiant answer precluded the possibility of God's wrapping His arms around one of His children to offer forgiveness and reconciliation.

God's question to Cain, though addressed in extreme circumstances, is one He is still asking us. We are responsible for our brother and his well-being. If hell is a state of total self-centeredness, then assuming responsibility for others is a way out of our hell. Adam and Eve disobeyed God and ate the fruit of the tree of knowledge because they wanted to be like God. They wanted to be in control. God designed us to love people and use things. Apart from Him we end up loving things and using people. Our brothers and sisters are important only as they fit into our plans and promote our well-being. Only as we make other people the objects of our love and concern do we begin to lose our self-centeredness.

The outline for this book came to me during my first (and, I hope, only) hospital stay. I was there for five days, having surgery for prostate cancer. Before that I had visited hospitals only as a pastor, seeing I suppose hundreds and hundreds of patients over the years. I was unaware of the subtle personality changes that can take place when you are the patient.

I had a remarkable recovery. I am not surprised, because so many people were praying for me. I shed more than one tear over the stacks of cards that came day after day from friends and old acquaintances. Even strangers wrote saying they had heard about my surgery and were concerned and were praying for me.

My doctor told me I was an outstanding patient. Most people with my surgery are hospitalized for seven days. I came home in five. On that last day, while waiting for my wife and son to come and take me home, I had an unsettling experience. Early in the morning the physician was removing my stitches (actually staples), preparing me to go home. In the middle of that procedure my breakfast arrived and was placed in a far corner of the room. When the doctor left, I realized my breakfast was getting cold, and, unable to get it myself, I asked, through the intercom, for a nurse to come and bring it to me. She said she was busy. A second call found her still busy. By the third call I found myself yelling for someone to please bring me my breakfast.

That's when I realized what had happened to me. In just five days I had become the center of my world. My pain, my medication, my catheter, my bowel movements, even my breakfast had become my whole focus. I realized what a ministry Christians can have to people in nursing homes or hospital situations. When you are a long-term patient it is so easy to become wrapped up in yourself. The only escape from that kind of total self-centeredness is to care for people around you and begin to serve them. That is the broader message in God's question to Cain.

The Christian life is a life of community. Jesus called twelve men to follow Him. I'm sure it wasn't long before each one realized that he was stuck with eleven other people with whom he had *not* chosen to live his life. Further, they were exhorted to love one another as Jesus loved them. It must have been a challenge as they ate together, slept together, and walked together every day for three years. But they learned that there can be no insular or solitary faith. As soon as we begin a relationship with God, He begins to move us in the direction of the people around us. His question to all of us is, "Where is your brother?"

My mother was a remarkable Christian by all standards. She gave her time and money and nurture to many people. Her church was the center of her life, and Jesus was the Lord of her life. But when her husband, my stepfather, died, she grieved for an unusually long time. I worried about her. But that all changed one day when a minister from her church asked her to become a part of a tutoring program for disadvantaged ghetto kids. She was assigned a young black girl named Rosemary, who came to see her several nights a week for help with reading. My mother, a former schoolteacher, began a relationship with Rosemary that extended beyond just tutoring. Rosemary blossomed and made great progress as a result of all the love and caring. And my mother found an outlet for her love that helped to fill the vacuum left by her husband's death. Rosemary was as much a gift from God to my mother as my mother was a gift from Him to Rosemary.

Life can change dramatically as we hear and respond to that question to Cain, "Where is your brother?" I have known a great many lay men and women over the years who experienced a turning point when they went out, scared but determined and at their own expense, on some cross-cultural mission. They were never the same once they had spent time living with some of the poorest of the poor in the third world. The jobs were unglamorous—doing manual labor to build orphanages or houses or schools, helping in hospitals, tending children. But by making a deliberate choice to get involved in the problems of others, they discovered a new awareness of God and His purposes in the world.

Just how responsible are we supposed to be for our brother? We hear a great deal these days about codependency, and we need to make it clear that many of us feel falsely responsible for the fact that a parent or a spouse or a child is addicted to some toxic substance or to destructive behavior, and we make excuses for them. Our cooperation makes it possible for the other person to continue in that damaging life-style. But God's question to Cain focuses on our responsibility to care for our brother in helpful and tangible ways.

We avoid that responsibility with all sorts of excuses. Let's look at some of them. We may say, as Cain did, "Why do you ask me about my brother? I am not involved with him." But in this global family we are all, to some degree, responsible for our brothers in the third world, in the inner city, or in our top boardrooms. It doesn't matter where they are. If they are members of the human race, we are involved with and affected by their welfare.

We can say, "What brother? I have hurt no one. I am minding my own business in life. I'm asking for nothing and giving nothing." This response reminds us of some of the people in the story Jesus told about the Good Samaritan. A man was attacked by thieves and beaten and robbed. They of course are the villains in the story. But equally guilty are the priest and the Levite who walk by and do nothing. They have pressing religious business and have no time to get involved with the injured man. They do nothing to hurt him, but neither do they do anything to help.

Another answer we might give to this question about our brother is that he is undeserving. He is shiftless and lazy and doesn't deserve our help. That was the attitude toward the poor of my parents and their friends, all of them immigrants. Those Swedes came to America with nothing in their pockets, worked hard, and made a decent living. They were contemptuous of anyone on welfare. They made it, and there must be something wrong with anyone who can't.

Today we are more aware of the deep-seated causes of powerlessness and poverty in our cities and in the world. But there are still those who feel that too many people are getting a free ride.

This concern may need to be addressed on a local, state, or national level, but what about the people God has directly put in our path? It's not always easy to try to sort out which of them is genuinely deserving.

God taught me a lasting lesson in my very first pastorate. It was a snowy Saturday morning just before Christmas, and there was a knock on the door of the parish house. We were living in a tiny apartment on the second floor with our two babies. On the doorstep was a middle-aged man, bedraggled and boozy. He introduced himself as the son of a couple in my congregation, and I immediately recalled their sad story. They had loved and supported and rescued him countless times and had finally, in despair, given up on him. He was no longer welcome at their home. He needed money. He needed food and warm clothes. He needed a place to stay. He needed a job. Would I help?

My mind was racing. I had a mountain of extra church duties in the Christmas season. I had calls to make and meetings to plan. I had family responsibilities. I found myself thinking at the end of this man's sad recital, "God, what do you want me to do? I can't take care of every drunk in this town." The answer came in a flash: "I didn't send you every drunk in town. Just this one." Of course I took him in. Eventually, I enlisted the help of the men in my weekly prayer group, and they managed to find him housing and a job, and even to keep him sober.

We may feel we are already helping our brother. We give to the United Way, the Red Cross. We're happy to send checks that will foster those programs that care for our brother. That is not a bad response, but it's not enough. It's a step removed from any personal involvement. But how encouraging to see someone like former President Carter and his wife, Rosalynn, picking up hammers and saws and helping to build houses for the poor through the Habitat for Humanity Ministry. God wants us to do more than write checks. Money can't take the place of that kind of personal involvement.

The truth is that a good many of our personal problems could be put in perspective, if not solved, by getting involved with other people's pain. Without this involvement a lot of people wind up materially successful, but unhappy and lonely. Tennessee Williams, who often dealt with the problems of loneliness and alienation in his plays, wrote, "If loneliness is as prevalent as we are led to believe that it is, then surely the great sin of our time must be to be lonely alone." That loneliness can be assuaged only as we reach out for our brother by praying for him, standing with him, weeping when he weeps, and rejoicing when he rejoices. In other words, caring for him as best we can.

One of the most memorable sermons I have heard Robert Schuller preach since I have been his co-pastor at the Crystal Cathedral was titled "Beyond Success to Significance." Somehow, it's not enough to be the CEO, the brilliant lawyer, the best teacher, even the multimillionaire. Consciously or unconsciously, we want to count. We want our lives to make a difference to others. We are meant to use our success to become significant.

Jesus gives us an opportunity to do that when He invites us to take up His cross and follow Him. The idea of taking up a cross has been seriously misunderstood by most Christians. A cross has nothing to do with unchosen suffering. It is not the unavoidable difficulties of life—illness, an alcoholic spouse, a wayward child. My bout with cancer was not a cross. I would never have chosen to have cancer. My little grandson, Samuel, died in utero, just two weeks before term. I would never have chosen his death. Suffering comes to all of us, and God helps us through it with His love and grace.

To take up our cross is to choose to enter into somebody else's problems, hurts, pains, and concerns. Dietrich Bonhoffer, German pastor martyred by the Nazis, once said, "To be a Christian is to suffer with God in a godless world." That's what we do when we take up our cross. We share in the loneliness and pain of others and try to make a difference.

On the other hand, we need to be aware that in some cases our efforts to help may end up supporting destructive behavior and encouraging it to continue. There is an alarming trend today to blame others for our problems, which we see as the result of an abusive father, an alcoholic mother, a deprived childhood. Violent crime is explained away by an unfortunate upbringing. Society has become the culprit for much that is wrong in the world.

This is the theme of a new book by Charles Sykes called A Nation of Victims. He tells some alarming tales. A New Yorker who jumped in front of a subway train while drunk is awarded $650,000 because the train hit him. An FBI employee fired for embezzling $2,000 is reinstated after a court rules that his affinity for gambling with other people's money is a handicap. A school-district employee fired for habitual lateness sues for reinstatement because chronic lateness is a disability.

How hard it is to say mea culpa even in our own lives. We maintain our innocence. Someone else must be to blame for our problems. We defend our actions and accuse others of insensitivity. This pattern crops up especially often in marriage. When my wife reacted angrily in some discussion, I would find myself saying, "All I said was . . . " For example, "All I said was, 'Is your mother coming to visit again?' Why did that make you angry?" You see the implication? I am the sane and reasonable person, and my wife reacts in a rage. I'm married to an emotional basket case!

A friend once cared enough to point out to me what the problem was. "Larson," he said, "you always judge yourself by your intentions and other people by their actions." He was right! You see, I am never wrong in anything I do because my intentions are always good, or I like to think they are. But I never give you the benefit of the doubt when it comes to your intentions. I judge you by the hurtful things you say and do. Since that revealing conversation, I have tried, with God's help, to change. I am trying to be a little harder on myself and a little more charitable about other people.

"Where is your brother?" The question has taken on particular meaning in these past fifty years as the world has become a global village. In the words of John Donne, "No man is an island." That has never been more true than in this time when every night, on the TV news, we are shown pictures of earthquake victims, cities ravaged by war, children starving. What I do and do not do affects my brothers and sisters all over the world. We may not, like Cain, have slain our brother, but by our indifference or uninvolvement, we are consenting to his death. But beyond admitting our complicity, as Cain did not do, we can begin to take actions that will change the way our brothers and sisters live. This is the pathway to significance and the doorway out of our own self-centeredness.

Let's keep in mind that we don't bring Christ to the world. We discover Him there! When Mother Teresa received the Nobel Prize she reacted in surprise. Her words were astonishing: "We need the poor more than the poor need us." She finds meaning and joy in caring for the dying on the streets of Calcutta. She invites us to join her.

Some of the heroes in my life are people who have heard the question, "Where is your brother?" and have taken it seriously. Ed and Marge in Garden Grove, California, head up a feeding program for the hungry and homeless in Orange County. Their lives have never been richer!

A woman now in retirement who used to sell high-fashion women's clothes has recruited her friends to make thousands of sandwiches a week for the street people in her city.

A couple of retired florists on an around-the-world trip on a tramp steamer were stabbed by the overwhelming problems of the Masai people in the Rift Valley of Kenya. The land has been partitioned and can no longer accommodate wandering cattle raisers. Unless the Masai change their life-style, find stable water supplies, and learn how to grow vegetables, they cannot survive. Denny and Jean Grindall were not trained missionaries, but they moved into a Masai village and lived there for over twenty years. They built dams, planted vegetable gardens, started schools and churches. I don't know of any two people more fulfilled than these two.

Another friend is the superintendent of schools in a major city. He inherited a system in disarray. Only a minority of the students were doing well—those who had parents who cared, who insisted that they study and do their homework. My friend speaks frequently to service clubs such as the Kiwanis, Rotary, and Lions, as well as to various church groups, and he began to ask for volunteers to help him change the schools. In five years he recruited twenty thousand people to work on a one-to-one basis with one student every week.

Phil is another hero. The owner of a car agency, he became president of his Rotary Club. The members had always given money to worthy causes, but Phil got them into hands-on service in some of the needier places in the city. They were required to report back weekly on their projects. For most of those men and women it was a new experience, and it was exhilarating.

St. Francis of Assisi was perhaps the first Roman Catholic clergyman to equate ministry with aggressive and personal caring for his brother. Francis was a multimillionaire, born to the manor. He gave away his wealth when he became a Christian, and he saw the world as his parish. He traveled extensively, caring for the poorest of the poor, lepers, prisoners, and slaves. His nickname was Joculator Domini, which means "the jolly priest."

A huge shrine has been built in Assisi over his bones, and some of his personal possessions are on display, including his undergarments. Great crowds come every day and stand in line, jostling each other to get a glimpse of the saint's underwear. St. Francis must be crying out from heaven in despair as he sees what's happening. Those artifacts are not his legacy. Rather, he gave us a model of what it means to care for our brothers and sisters in a way that leads to hilarious joy.

Perhaps one of the reasons we don't respond to the question, "Where is your brother?" is the fear that we will be taken advantage of or hurt by those we're trying to help. We fear we will find ourselves sacrificing money and time and energy to help somebody, only to discover we are being ripped off. That's certainly a possibility.

Roberto de Vincenzo is a well-known professional golfer, and on one occasion he won a seniors' tournament. His prize was a check for several thousand dollars. On the way to his car he was approached by a woman who appeared to be in some distress. She said she understood he was a man of compassion. Her daughter was ill with cancer and needed surgery, and she had no money or insurance. Would he please help her? Immediately he slapped his winning check on the hood of his car and signed it over to her.

Some friends who were with him at the time were troubled by this incident. They hired an investigator to research her story and eventually came to de Vincenzo with the results. The woman was a phony. There was no daughter with cancer. "No daughter with cancer?" he repeated. "No daughter with cancer? Why, that's the best news I've heard in a long time!"

God does not mete out His grace only to the deserving. That's why it's called grace. Someone has said that getting what we deserve is called justice. Not getting what we deserve is mercy. But getting what we don't deserve—that's grace.

CHAPTER THREE

"What Is That in Your Hand?"

THERE IS A TRUE STORY from the last century about a Portuguese sailing ship that ran out of water off the coast of South America. Many days went by, and the crew and passengers were suffering terribly when a second ship appeared on the horizon. The Portuguese ship was able to send a message describing its predicament and asking for help. The reply came back: "Lower your buckets." It seems they were floating at the mouth of the Amazon, where all the water is fresh.

In the same way, most of us already possess unexpected resources, and that is the thrust of a question God put to Moses, that monumental Old Testament figure who led the Israelites out of Egypt. God asked him, "What is that in your hand?"

Moses' early history is the stuff of novels. When Pharaoh instituted a mass slaughter of the male infants of the Hebrews, Moses' mother hid him near a stream where Pharaoh's daughter bathed. Moses was found by the princess and taken into her household to be raised. But when he was grown he went out among his own people, and upon seeing an overseer beating one of them, he impulsively killed the Egyptian. He was forced to flee for his own life and settled in the Midian Desert.

That's where God encountered him many years later. Moses first heard God speak to him from the flames of a burning bush. A bush exploding into flame is not unusual in the desert. The intense heat ignites combustible properties. But in this case, the fire did not consume the bush. That's what first got Moses' attention. He was then called by name and given a commission—to lead God's people out of Egypt.

Moses' reaction was hardly enthusiastic. He started to enumerate all the reasons he was not the person for this task. God knew he was hiding out in the Midian Desert because he was wanted for murder in Egypt. How could he go back and free the Hebrews? Why should they follow him? How could he convince them that God had sent him? Besides, he was no speaker. He had no equipment for this job.

In the midst of those protestations, God asked one of the great questions of the Bible: "What is that in your hand?" Moses was holding what any good shepherd would be holding—a rod used to guide the sheep.

If we speculate on God's choice of Moses for this awesome task, we see that Moses had some special qualifications. First of all, he had been living among the bedouins for forty years, caring for the sheep entrusted to him. He was uniquely prepared to lead the Israelites through a killing, punishing desert that showed no mercy toward men or animals.

Trained to lead sheep, Moses had also been conditioned to deal with the perversity of human nature. He would discover that God's people—all of us—are very much like sheep. We are dumb and stubborn and difficult to lead. We get lost. We get frightened.

Furthermore, Moses had special access to Pharaoh's household. He had been raised there, and he understood the politics of the court and knew its people. All in all, he had just the background and experience to undertake the commission God was giving him.

God's call to Moses was frighteningly dramatic. His call to us may be quieter, in a still, small voice, through a book or a sermon. But when we hear Him calling us to a particular work, we usually come up with all sorts of reasons why it isn't possible, just as Moses did. "But, Lord, I'm not smart enough; I need more schooling. I haven't studied theology [or psychology or sociology or medicine]." Or we say, "Lord, I don't have the financial resources to start helping people in your name. I would need to win the lottery or have some rich relative die and leave me money." Or "Lord, I'm not in the right place. My job is too insignificant to really count in this work for you." That last complaint is the refuge of a lot of us clergy types. We think we need a bigger church or a more prominent church or a more loving church to accomplish something great for God.

The question that God asked Moses was designed to help him and us discover that we already have the resources needed to do the job. God will use whatever is in our hand. We need not begin to look for more credentials or more money or a more prestigious platform. We can begin with what we do have.

During my years in Seattle as the pastor of University Presbyterian Church, I met a remarkable man. His name is Rich Walsh, and he is a quadriplegic. His arms and legs are useless. He can move only his head, and he steers his wheelchair with his chin. He was injured in a car accident with his brother at the wheel. Before that catastrophe struck, he had been a wealthy builder, successful in every way. At age forty Rich became a quadriplegic, cared for by public assistance.

More than anything else in the world Rich wanted independence, but our protective society refused to let him live on his own. He literally had to fight his way out of a free-care center. His counselor tried to discourage him by pointing out the problems: "Rich, if you wake up in the middle of the night and your nose itches, who's going to scratch it for you?"; "If you're cold and want the window closed, who will close it for you?" But Rich persisted and began life on his own. Further, with his intimate knowledge of the needs of seriously handicapped people, he started something called the Resource Center for the Handicapped. It was and continues to be one of the most remarkable schools for the training of seriously handicapped people.

I've visited the center many times and have even used it as the subject of a television project. Boeing, Microsoft, and any number of other leading corporations in the Seattle area send their best computer trainers there to teach. They have found that some of the most seriously handicapped people are amazingly bright and are perfectly able to do computer work. At graduation time many companies bid top salaries to lure the center's graduates.

Rich Walsh has done the impossible. The equipment in his hand was simply his own situation. He understood the needs of seriously handicapped people. I've heard him say that had it not been for his handicap, he would never have had a life of significance. His tragedy became a tool of liberation for others and continues to be that to this day.

A certain man from Tennessee was outraged that so many Americans are hungry while food is being thrown away at our hotels and restaurants and grocery stores every day. He set up an organization to tap into that resource, and it currently provides about sixty thousand meals daily with no staff and no overhead. What did this man have in his hand? Just his concern and his determination to change things.

I serve as co-pastor of one of the great churches in Christendom, but our founding pastor, Robert Schuller, seemed to have very little in his hand when he began his ministry thirty-eight years ago. He was sent out by the Reformed Church in America with five hundred dollars to start a church in Orange County. He soon found that there were almost no people of his denomination living in the area. Since he hadn't inherited a denominational group with a particular tradition, he simply knocked on doors to find out what it was people in the area needed. In those early years, there was no church building. Worship was held at a drive-in movie theater. Dr. Schuller and his wife hauled the organ there each Sunday on the back of a truck, and she played it herself. Thus began a church of positive thinkers, and the shadow of that church now extends across the nation and across the world.

What did Robert Schuller have in his hand? Unwavering faith and a positive belief that God was going to do something new and significant.

A former parishioner of mine, a veterinarian, wanted nothing so much as to be a missionary caring for animals all over the third world. He did not meet all the requirements and couldn't pass the physical. Deeply disappointed, he began to look around his own city for an opportunity to serve. He and his wife hit upon the idea of starting a free clinic for the pets of street people. He ran that clinic one day a week for several years, and he treated an amazing assortment of animals who were sharing life on the streets with their owners—dogs, cats, birds, even a hermit crab.

This veterinarian died of cancer a few years ago, and on the day of his funeral our church was filled with street people and their pets. It's the only occasion I know of when dogs and cats were allowed in the sanctuary! What did Bud Doney have in his hand? His skills as a veterinarian and the desire to use those skills to make life better for some segment of society.

We can spend a lot of time and energy looking and waiting for the right resources. I used to head up a lay renewal mission in New York City. During those years I met with a group of men for lunch once a week. We would talk about our faith, read the Bible, and pray for each other. Apart from me, they were all businessmen. One man had a special concern about the problems and pressures of businesspeople in our midtown area.

Wouldn't it be wonderful if Christian men and women had a quiet place to go in the midst of the hubbub to pray? His scheme was to try to raise money to rent a room that could be used as a chapel. One noon another lunch-club member, a commercial artist, announced that he had found a solution. "Irv," he said, "I have found your chapel. As a matter of fact, I have found twenty thousand chapels all over Manhattan. They are Bell telephone booths." He continued, "The other day I was having a hard time with a customer. I stepped out into the hall and into the phone booth. I closed the door and took the phone off the hook. I could talk to God freely there, and no one bothered me or even noticed me. Think of it. God already has chapels all over the city. Just pop into a phone booth and talk to God."

Sometimes we need to see our problems with fresh insight and a new perspective. That's what the boy David did when he met the giant Goliath. Goliath, you recall, was the champion of the Philistine army, and he challenged anyone in Saul's army to do battle with him. All the Israelites, including their king, were terrified of this savage warrior. David was still a boy, not even a soldier. He was on the scene bringing lunch to his brothers, who were in the army. "Let me have a whack at him," he said. The soldiers were skeptical: "Goliath is so big we can't possibly beat him." David had a different view: "Goliath is so big, I can't possibly miss." The king offered to give David his armor, thinking he did not have the right equipment for this battle. David said, "I cannot go with these, for I am not used to them." Instead, he gathered five smooth stones; his sling was already in his hand. You know the rest of the story. With the very first stone, David won the day.

It is often in our weaknesses that we find God's strength both to help ourselves and to help others. At the Crystal Cathedral we have dozens and dozens of support groups for every conceivable kind of human condition. There are divorce support groups and cancer support groups. There are support groups for every kind of addiction—alcohol, drugs, sex, overeating. There are grief support groups for new widows and widowers. The list goes on and on. The leaders of all these groups are people who have had those problems. "What is in your hand?" Your addictions, your cancer, your divorce, your overeating, or whatever, when given to God, becomes your equipment for ministry. Jesus said, "My power is made perfect in weakness" (2 Cor. 12:9).

If you are a Christian and you are being called to ministry, you can be sure God has already equipped you for that ministry. What is in your hand right now? Before you look for other resources, let's take an inventory. Here are six things that all of us have that God can use to help and bless others.

1. Your pain. Any pain that you have been through—physical, emotional, mental, relational, financial—gives you credentials. If you have been there, you have authority to speak to someone else in pain.

2. Your forgiven sins. The sins that you have committed against God, yourself, or others have produced a sense of humility. You don't judge other people. You have empathy with those who are failing in some area. This principle is at work in AA—where alcoholics help other alcoholics to get sober and stay sober.

3. Your mistakes. That may seem an unusual resource, but every dumb thing that you have ever done ought to have produced wisdom. You've learned a better way to live. Those of us who have done enough foolish things and learned from them are a source of hope and encouragement for others.

4. Your expertise. God has given us all particular talents. If you've had years of training in some field, of course that can be

used. Perhaps your talents are less easily identified. But whether they're relational, organizational, or whatever, they are part of what is currently in your hand to be used for ministry.

5. Your connections. Unless you are extremely dysfunctional, there are people who know you and love you and respect you and trust you. I'm talking about your colleagues, friends, neighbors; the people in your church, your lodge, your union. Among that larger group is a core that you could call on for help and they would respond. Whether that power base of relationships is large or small, it is a primary asset for ministry. We are accustomed to thinking of the wealthy and privileged as having a power base, but even the poor have one they can make work for them.

My daughter is a legal-services attorney in Florida. She was concerned about many of the decisions being handed down by a local judge. She felt they were often biased and sometimes even racist. She recruited some of the women in her community who were senior citizens and unemployed to show up in the judge's courtroom every day. They sat there faithfully for a number of weeks. The judge, disconcerted by these people who appeared for no known reason every day, began to make some more-enlightened decisions. He didn't know that most of the women could not speak any English. Their presence was a force that made him accountable. Sometimes we can exert our power simply by being present.

6. Your reputation. If you have spent most of your life being honest and industrious, caring and kind, then you have built up a whole lot of moral capital. If you were to take a stand for

something or ask for help for some cause, people who know you would have to take you seriously. Unfortunately, when we die our moral capital dies with us. We cannot transfer this to anybody else. We can pass our financial capital on to our children. (Though I hope you're not planning to leave a lot of money behind. I hope you've given it away, invested it, or spent it and had the fun of seeing it work for God.) But your moral capital cannot be transmitted. Start drawing on it. Before you die, use it to gain support for causes you care about.

Those are just some of the resources all of us already have in our hands, but we may be uncertain of how we can go about using them. In my last parish, our congregation was given a challenge to "love Seattle." People who wanted to become involved in some specific ministry to their city were asked to come to church one particular Sunday evening. Over one thousand people showed up. They were sorted out into different groups according to their responses to two questions: What kind of people do you most enjoy being with? What kind of work or ministry would you most like to do?

The results turned up some surprises. Some young people preferred to work with older people rather than their own peers. Some men felt uncomfortable in men-only groups. There's no way to predict how people will define their own comfort zone. The second question came out of the belief that God doesn't want you in some ministry you don't enjoy. In any field—teaching, medicine, business, preaching—we are at our best when we are enthusiastic about what we do. Still, many were startled by the idea that ministry could mean working with the kinds of people you enjoy, doing the kinds of things you like to do.

We pastors had no specific programs in mind. But as people formed groups of anywhere from three to forty they began to discover all kinds of creative ways to become involved with the city. Many of those ministries continue today, and their impact has been significant. Those who got involved were simply using what was already in their hand.

But before we can launch into ministry using whatever we have at hand, we often have to overcome some major blocks. Perhaps these three are the most pervasive:

1. We believe we are trapped by our circumstances. We are victims of wrong choices, stupid actions, and poor relationships, and therefore we are hopeless.

2. We doubt our dreams. Faced with an opportunity to act for God in the life of another, we say, like Moses, "I could never do that; that's not possible. I'm not equipped."

3. We rely on our instincts. But instinctively we act out of self-interest, out of our need for self-preservation and security. That's the message we've gotten from well-meaning parents and teachers and pastors and friends. Play it safe. Take care of yourself. Jesus' advice to us is a radical departure from that: "If you save your life you lose it, if you lose it for my sake you'll find it" (Matt. 16:25).

"What is that in your hand?" In Moses' case, a simple instrument he used every day in his job as a shepherd would be used by God to help in liberating a nation. We've talked about six things each of us is already holding—our pain, our forgiven sins, our expertise, our connections, our reputation, and even our mistakes. When the church was born at Pentecost the Holy Spirit came as promised so that "young men shall see visions and old men shall dream dreams" (Acts 2:17). With that Spirit in us, we are all dreamers, young and old, male and female. Believe that the resources are already in your hand to make those dreams a reality.

CHAPTER FOUR

"Who Will Go for Us?"

I'VE OFTEN WONDERED what would happen if, during worship some Sunday, I should announce that God Himself would be in church the next week with a specific message for each person there. Would the place be packed? Certainly we come each week expecting to meet God, but would that kind of dramatic and direct encounter be too terrifying? The prophet Isaiah had just such an experience.

It was a time of trouble, the year in which King Uzziah died. Israel had many kings, some wonderful, some terrible, and some simply mediocre. But Uzziah was a great and wise king whose death left a leadership vacuum and a spiritual malaise.

Isaiah, in this dark hour, continued to exercise his faith. While the nation was mourning the death of King Uzziah, the faithful continued to worship God in His temple, and Isaiah was one of those worshipers. He had an unusual experience. He saw a vision of God "high and lifted up and His train filled the temple."

This vision of God immediately produced a sense of unworthiness in Isaiah, an awareness of sin. When two seraphim appeared to announce that this was the Lord of Hosts, Isaiah's

reaction was: "Woe is me! I am ruined! For I am a man of unclean lips and I live among a people of unclean lips and my eyes
have seen the King, the Lord almighty." To encounter God and
see Him as He really is is to be overwhelmed by a sense of our
own unworthiness and impurity.

God took the initiative in the encounter with Isaiah. A coal
was removed from the altar by one of the seraphim, who
touched Isaiah's mouth with it. God said, "See, this has
touched your lips. Your guilt is taken away and your sin forgiven." Isaiah could do nothing to make himself worthy to
stand in God's presence. It is God who enables cleansing and
reconciliation.

Then Isaiah was given a challenge—a task: "Whom shall I
send and who will go for us?" It is this question we are considering in this chapter, and it is a "next step" question for all serious Christians. We are called to go about our Father's
business.

Isaiah responded to the call immediately and positively:
"Here am I. Send me." And God said to go and speak for Him
to the people. It is the commission given to the company of
the faithful, beginning with the patriarch Abraham and continuing on through to the first disciples, to the apostle Paul, and
to all those since who have obeyed that call.

Isaiah's experience demonstrates the six stages of any authentic Christian experience. We feel a need. We turn to God.
We are overwhelmed by our own unworthiness. We are
cleansed through God's initiative. We are asked to go and tell.
We respond. In doing so, we take our place among all those
past and present who have accepted God's commission.

Religion generally focuses on our feelings of unworthiness, struggling to bridge the gap between a perfect and holy and just God and imperfect and sinful man. How do the unclean become clean? How do the unworthy become worthy? How does someone with a bent nature become a good and righteous person? The church often takes a legalistic approach to the problem. How much must I do? How many candles must I light? How many prayers must I say? How much must I deny my basic instincts? How much must I reform my life? How much must I deny myself pleasures? How much must I study and learn? How much must I give financially?

God's presence inevitably shines a light on our own unworthiness, the dark and shabby parts of our lives. But Isaiah's experience gives us fresh insight into God's nature and His willingness to make the relationship possible. God knows we cannot make ourselves righteous or worthy. He will take care of that if we trust Him. That was the experience of the apostle Peter. When this Jesus to whom he had loaned his boat was able to command fish to appear in the net, he understood that he was in God's presence. He said, as Isaiah did, "Depart from me for I am a sinful man." Not only does Jesus not depart from Peter, sinful as he is; He calls him into service.

"Who will go for us?" We are sometimes reluctant to respond to the call because we believe God wants perfection. We get overfocused on our own mixed motives and bad intentions and poor performance. It's possible to squander our lives in riotous self-justification. But God can use imperfect vessels. That's all He has. Martin Luther, that great reformer, once said, "Love God and sin boldly." He was not advocating license and irresponsible living. Rather, he was urging us not to make the avoidance of evil the focus of our lives, but instead to accept the fact that we're going to fail in more than one area no matter how hard we try. As Christians we *are* trying, but our focus needs to be on loving God and serving Him with our whole heart. We can trust Him with our past, present, and even future sins.

King David, one of the genuine rascals of the Old Testament narrative, was a liar, a thief, an adulterer, and a murderer. Nevertheless, God called him "a man after my own heart." King David understood God's grace. He confessed his sins. He repented. He claimed forgiveness, and he wanted with all his heart to serve God.

As for Peter, he did not always succeed in the commission Jesus gave him. At the time of Jesus' arrest and trial, he denied Him three times, fearful for his own safety. However, in a post-Resurrection appearance Jesus joined Peter at the seaside. Their dialogue is significant. Peter had run away and gone back to fishing. Knowing of Peter's cowardice and betrayal, Jesus asked him the same question three times: "Peter, do you love me?" Peter answered first, "Lord, you know that I love you." The second time he repeated, "Lord, you know I love you." The third time, sounding a little impatient, Peter said, "Yes, Lord, you know all things. You know I love you." To each of those declarations of love, Jesus responded with the same answer: "Feed my sheep." If we love Him, we make His agenda our agenda, and He is still asking us to feed His sheep. That means entering into the suffering and pain and injustice of others and helping them.

Our call is to adventure and not to some problem-free existence. I had lunch a while back with a young pastor who was leaving a large church to accept a new call. He was going to a very small church in a country town, and he was looking forward to the relative peace he expected in that two-hundred-member congregation.

I said, "Well, lots of luck. But if you succeed there, it won't be a two-hundred-member church for long."

I understand his longing for that simple life. It's a romantic idea. I sometimes fantasize that I am a St. Francis type, walking in my garden in the morning, wearing my bathrobe like the statues we see of the saint. I stand in the garden holding out birdseed, and the birds fly down to eat out of my hand. I wave at the squirrels. I hear two little boys fighting next door. Man of God that I am, I go out and say, "Now, boys, don't you know God loves you? Can't you make up and be friends?" They say, "Why, of course," and they are reconciled. Later, I call on the sick and lay hands on them, and they bless me.

We all have a romantic idea of what it means to be a Christian, a person of faith. The biblical view is quite different from that. In truth, the life of Francis wasn't all that romantic, either. He traveled the world caring for the poor, the outcasts, the lepers, giving any worldly possessions he had to anyone in need. God's call was to a life of uncertainty and deprivation.

When Jesus told the apostle Peter three times to feed His sheep, He continued the dialogue with a prophesy: "Peter, you will stretch out your hands and another will gird you and carry you where you do not wish to go" (John 21:18). In other words, "In the future you will go where I lead you and not where you want to go. I will direct how you live, where you live, what you do, and where you go."

"Who will go for us?" We may not always accept that call or perform that service gladly, but Jesus told a parable that indicates that our willingness, or lack of it, is sometimes beside the point. A certain man had two sons. He gave them each a task. One said, to put it in the vernacular, "Sure, Pop, I'll be glad to do it!" But he did nothing. The other son said, "Why me? How about my brother? It's his turn to do it." But he ended up doing it. Which son, Jesus asks, serves the father better? Our obedience and our actions are more important than our attitude.

Even if we are willing to accept God's commission, the average preacher or a typical worship service does not always provide us with the impetus. Buckner Fanning, the pastor of the First Baptist Church of San Antonio, tells about a conversation he had with a parishioner early on in his ministry. They were talking about Buckner's preaching and his attempt to give some kind of inspirational message. Suddenly the parishioner turned to him and said, "Preacher, I have all the inspiration I need. Please give me a handle!" I think that man was speaking for a great many people in the pews today: "Tell me how I can begin to serve God and make a difference in His world."

One of my favorite stories about Abraham Lincoln concerns his response to a sermon he heard during his White House years. He often slipped into the Wednesday-night service at New York Avenue Presbyterian Church, where a Dr. Gurley was the pastor. In order not to disrupt things, he would listen from the privacy of the pastor's study, which adjoined the sanctuary.

A young aide usually came along, and on one particular night he asked Lincoln how he liked the sermon. "I thought it was well thought through, powerfully delivered, and very eloquent," was the reply. "Then you thought it was a great sermon?" the young man continued. "No," said Lincoln, "it failed. It failed because Dr. Gurley did not ask us to do something great." Lincoln understood that in meaningful worship we ought to hear God's call—the same kind of call Isaiah heard: "Who will go for us?"

Whether or not we are physically able to go for Him, as Isaiah was asked to do, we can go into the world with our money. If God truly owns us and all that we have, then we ought to be happy to return a tenth. That's an extreme step for a lot of Christians. A poem I saw in an Atlanta church bulletin put it this way:

Oh, God—
The bumper sticker says smile if you love Jesus;
So I smiled all day long . . .
And people thought I worked for Jimmy Carter.
The bumper sticker said honk if you love Jesus;
So I honked . . . and a policeman arrested me
For disturbing the peace in a hospital zone.
The bumper sticker said wave if you love Jesus;
So I waved with both hands . . . but lost control of
    the car
And crashed into the back of a Baptist bus.
Oh, God—
If I cannot smile . . . or honk . . . or wave . . .
How will Jesus know I love Him . . . ?
IF YOU LOVE JESUS, TITHE . . . HONKING IS
    TOO EASY.

Few people know that John D. Rockefeller was a tither. He became one of the richest men in the world and founded the Standard Oil Company. It's estimated he gave away over $500 million to philanthropic enterprises in his lifetime. He built Riverside Church in New York, Rockefeller Chapel at the University of Chicago, dozens of hospitals, and hundreds of schools for education and social-aid programs.

You may think it's easy for a man of wealth to tithe, but Rockefeller's own testimony, given in 1932, tells a different story: "I have tithed on every dollar that God entrusted unto me, and I want to say to you that I could never have tithed on my first million if I had not tithed on my first salary which was $1.50 a week. Whether God would entrust me with little or with much, in the beginning, I did not know. I only knew that what I made was actually God's and for Him to let me have most of it was a very generous deal."

God wants us to invest our money and our creativity and our ideas and our life for Him. Even George Bernard Shaw, certainly no Christian, understood the wisdom of that course. He once said, "Use your health, even to the point of wearing it out. That is what it is for. Spend all you have before you die; and do not outlive yourself." That's good advice from a secularist.

There have been so many moving examples of men and women through the ages who have responded to God's question, "Who will go for us?" with Isaiah's answer, "Here I am. Send me." My life has been enriched by some of the people in my own generation who have similarly answered that call.

When my friend Millard Fuller first dreamed of building houses for the poorest of the poor all over the world, I confess I thought him an impractical dreamer. Since then Habitat for Humanity has been born. Tens of thousands of families live in houses that they could never have afforded, because one man gave us a dream and motivated us.

Another friend is retired and lives in Orange County, California, on a disability pension. His hobby is fishing, and one day Bernie Dailey realized how many fish went to waste. Much of his catch and that of other pleasure boaters was simply thrown away. He organized a project called Fishing for the Poor. With the gift of a used van, Bernie has collected tens of thousands of pounds of fish over the last two years. They go to feeding stations all over Orange County.

Then there's John Fling, who grew up in Gabbottville, Georgia—population forty-six. His parents were too poor to qualify as sharecroppers. They were sharecroppers' helpers. At age twenty-five, after a six-year stint in the U.S. Army, John settled with his wife in Columbia, South Carolina. He landed a job supervising one hundred boys who delivered newspapers. He began to care for those boys and their families with food, clothing, and school supplies, and he encouraged others to help him in this very personal mission. John and his wife have never owned a home. They now live on Social Security in a rent-free cottage. Though he's worked all his life, sometimes at several jobs at once, John has very few material possessions.

He is now retired, but John Fling still spends most of his waking hours, as he has for forty-five years, driving the streets of Columbia looking for someone to help. He delivers food, medicine, and laundry. He helps with bills, repairs screen doors, mows lawns, unstops sinks, transports the needy to appointments. His extended family includes two hundred seniors, four hundred children, and forty blind people. He has a special concern for the blind, having lost the sight in one eye in a boyhood hunting accident. John has learned how to live. He is consumed by a passion to do God's work in the world.

Nevertheless, it's easy to get sidetracked from that primary calling. We can get caught up in endless self-help programs or doctrinal disputes. Eschatology—beliefs about the end of the world—provides one arena for such disputes. Sometimes I think this focus on understanding the last days has to be part of some dark plot to divert the energies of well-intentioned people.

A new book called *Apocalypse Now,* by John Noe, reminds us that Jesus said, in regard to predicting the last days, "About that day and hour no one knows." We are not to believe anyone who says he or she knows. So many people are deflected from the simple command that God gave Isaiah or Jesus gave Peter and are instead absorbed by the timing of the end of the world. Where is Armageddon? Who will be fighting in that battle? When will the Lord come again? All this unprofitable speculation siphons off our energies from the clear and direct question God asks: "Who will go for us?"

Our only hope for the future lies with those who respond as Isaiah did: "Here am I. Send me."

CHAPTER FIVE

"Do You Want to Be Well?"

AT A RECENT family reunion, I heard a wonderful true story from my daughter. Her sister-in-law is a conservationist, and she and her husband and young son were driving up the coast of Florida on a vacation. They noticed a sign saying Naturist Camp and assumed that was the same as a naturalist camp. They drove in, parked their car, and headed toward the beach. They quickly realized that this naturist camp was actually a nudist camp when they came upon a group of people, all stark naked, cycling along the beach. Their five-year-old son stopped and stared in amazement. "Look, Mom and Dad," he said, pointing, "they're not wearing safety helmets." Their obvious condition went unnoticed. This child had other expectations—in this case, if you ride a bicycle you'd better be properly protected.

Our expectations are a powerful shaping force in all the areas of our lives, particularly our health. That's why the question we'll be considering here is so pertinent. "Do you want to be well?" is how Jesus phrased it, and it was addressed to a paralyzed man who had been an invalid for thirty-eight years.

There is so much research being done today in the area of the interrelatedness of our emotions, our attitudes, our expectations, and our health. Jesus, in His pointed question, reveals His understanding of this interrelatedness.

We are now in the New Testament, and although the question is asked by Jesus, it is still in the category of questions God asks. The basis of my faith and that of orthodox Christendom is that Jesus is God. He says, "Whoever has seen me has seen the Father. I and the Father am one" (John 14:7–11). The question Jesus put to the paralyzed man seems an odd one. It is "Do you *want* to be well?" But let's examine the setting in which this was asked.

Jesus was strolling by the pool of Bethesda, a pool known for its healing properties. (That pool still exists in Jerusalem, although two thousand years of building and silt have left it far below current ground level.) People with all sorts of diseases gathered there because it was believed that from time to time an angel troubled the waters. When that happened, the first person in received healing.

We might at first consider this belief somewhat primitive, but we still have healing shrines today, including the famous one at Lourdes. People visit those places expecting a miracle. Some receive one, it would seem, and some do not, for reasons we can't explain.

In passing the pool, Jesus saw the man to whom He addressed this question, both timeless and timely: "Do you want to be well?"

The man must have been perplexed. The answer seems so

obvious. Why else would he have been lying there for thirty-eight years hoping for a miracle from these sacred waters?

In answer to Jesus' question the paralyzed man protested that he was a victim of the carelessness or indifference or inefficiency of family or friends. In thirty-eight years they had never gotten him into the pool in time. But he must have indicated his willingness to be healed, for Jesus said, "Take up your bed and walk." The man did so.

The story is intriguing and a source of great hope for all of us. When God walked the earth as a man He offered healing. In the case of this man who had been afflicted for so long, there was no attempt to review either his worthiness or his faith. Did he deserve God's special attention? It is not even an issue. The man needed only to be willing. Jesus demonstrated not only His love but His eagerness to bring restoration and health.

"Do you want to be well?" From that one question we could write a whole theology of grace. God is not just our Creator and our Redeemer. He wants to release His power into our lives and make us whole, but we need to be willing.

The paralytic's response to Jesus' question strikes a familiar note. Offered healing by this strange prophet whom he does not know, he gives an answer that sounds defensive. Rather than replying with a straight yes or no, he indicates that his condition is not his fault. His friends and family have failed him. His answer, you'll notice, has nothing to do with the question asked. He implies, as Adam and Cain did, that he is a victim in life and, further, that he is unloved and uncared-for.

God wants to give us wellness or wholeness, to make us what we are meant to be. But we are such defensive, guilt-ridden, complicated people that we cannot respond easily to God's simple offer.

Jesus is still asking us, "Do you want to be well?" Does the question seem odd? Would someone who is sick physically or morally or spiritually or mentally or relationally not want to be well? Given our free will, we always have choices.

On the verge of death, Moses gave the people he had led for forty years a challenge. "This day I call heaven and earth as witnesses against you that I have set before you life and death, blessings and curses. Now choose life, so that you and your children may live and that you may love the Lord your God, listen to His voice and hold fast to Him. For the Lord is your life . . ." (Deut. 30:19). Moses must have known that many, if not most, of our circumstances in life are chosen. When we choose God we choose life, and we begin to change the way we live, our behavior and our attitudes—our life-style, in fact.

And how much we've heard about that over the past decade. We drink too much, work too hard, exercise too little, engage in casual sex. We are caught up in all sorts of unrewarding relationships, surrounded by people who don't love us enough or appreciate us enough. We make unhealthy choices and then blame others for our situation. Either we can consider ourselves victims of the insensitivity of others, or we can make better choices. Choice is the issue. God is not on trial! His eagerness and willingness to help us and His great power to do so are established.

One doctor I know described a longtime patient who suddenly arrived in his office with crippling rheumatoid arthritis. Her hands had doubled up like claws almost overnight. After a thorough examination he asked her to sit down for a chat. He asked, "Has anything unusual happened to you recently?" "Oh, yes," she replied, "I know exactly what you mean, and furthermore I have no intention of forgiving him!" Hearing the story, I asked, "Forgive who?" The doctor said, "I have no idea, but she knew clearly who it was." Apparently, at that point in her life, nurturing a resentment was more important to her than her health.

It's been proposed that in some cases heart-attack patients have died willingly and eagerly because they saw death as the only way out of a difficult situation. Caught in a web of dishonesty or deceit or an impossible situation, they unconsciously sent a message to the heart to stop beating. They chose an honorable way out of a distasteful future.

Dr. Bernie Segal, in his book *Love, Medicine and Miracles,* tells about an illuminating experience with his patients. He is a pioneer in holistic medicine and the attitudinal factors in health. As a teaching Yale surgeon he sent a letter out to one hundred of his cancer patients saying, "If you want to learn how to live longer and better, come to my house on Wednesday evening for a visit. There'll be no charge. We'll talk about some things I'm discovering that will help you."

He was certain that each of his hundred patients would bring a friend or a family member and the house would be packed. Just twelve people showed up. That experience taught him a great deal about how our choices and our expectations shape the outcome of our illnesses.

A distant relative of mine who smoked constantly and drank excessively was told by his doctor that if he didn't stop he'd be dead in six months. He retorted in no uncertain terms that he'd rather live six months drinking and smoking than fifty more years abstaining. In fact, he died in just three months. His case is extreme, but he understood his choices. To his detriment, he insisted on living the remainder of his life on his own terms.

The unspoken message in Jesus' question is that we sometimes must pay a price to be well. We may refuse to choose wellness because of the benefits of having an illness. The man by the pool of Bethesda did not have to work. Somebody carried him down to the pool each day, where he could lie in the shade and hear all the local gossip. His infirmity may have entitled him to special privileges at home. Privilege and power often gravitate to the chronically ill person by virtue of the fact that he or she is not expected to compete.

I broke my leg once in a skiing accident. I traveled the country for six weeks with it in a cast, keeping my speaking engagements. My situation had real perks. The airlines arranged to drive me from plane to plane; I got to board first and was given a desirable seat.

But best of all, all my failures were forgiven. If the speech was not my best, or even if I bombed out, people were kind. Invariably someone would say, "Aren't you wonderful to come here and stand on that broken leg and speak to us." I found my handicap to be an advantage, and that could have become addictive.

We may avoid God's question believing that we are powerless to help ourselves. The man by the pool implied that he was powerless, and that is a myth for any of us. Everybody has some degree of power and can choose to use it. Some years ago I visited a doctor for a thorough checkup. After endless tests, the great man received me, examined all my charts, and pronounced me reasonably well for a man my age. Glancing at the record of my weight, he asked me a surprising question: "What do you want to weigh?" I was caught off guard. I felt like saying, "What do I want to weigh? You're the doctor; you tell me what I should weigh." Then it dawned on me that he was smart enough not to make my weight his problem. I stammeringly told him I wanted to weigh maybe ten, fifteen pounds less, and he said, "I'd like to help you with that." He came on board as my partner, not as a taskmaster with whom I could engage in a continuing struggle about my weight.

The myth of powerlessness has permeated so many areas of life in these last years. But to make those better choices we've been talking about, we need to move beyond that. Sigmund Freud and his whole approach to psychoanalysis was the starting point for the view that we are the hapless products of our early years. He stressed the need to examine and understand how all those childhood traumas have affected us before we can feel better about ourselves.

Fritz Perls, a very controversial psychologist and the founder of Gestalt psychology, said, "Psychoanalysis is a disease masquerading as a cure." He has a point. Psychoanalysis suggests that we are the result of what our parents have done to us in the early years and that at best we can make some accommodation to that. We are locked into our old patterns. On the other hand,

Erik Erickson, perhaps Freud's most brilliant disciple, empha-
sized that we can transcend our childhood to a very large extent. We have the power to choose who and what we will be.

Carl Rogers, one of the most innovative psychologists in
this half of the twentieth century and the father of nondirec-
tive counseling, said recently that he considers only one kind of
counselee relatively hopeless: the person who blames other
people for his or her problems. He claims that if you can own
the mess you're in, there is hope for you and help available.
That might be the intent of that question Jesus asked the man
by the pool of Bethesda: "Do you want to be well?"

Dr. Martin Seligman is the author of a book called *Learned
Optimism*. In it, this respected psychologist says that we all
have in our hearts a *yes* or a *no*. We respond to life either nega-
tively or positively. Seligman's thesis is that we can learn to put
a *yes* in our hearts. Doing so can change the course of our lives.

When I counsel someone whose marriage is in trouble, my
first question is always, "Tell me, do you want this marriage to
work? If you do, God has many ways to help you and your mate
to fall in love again and go beyond where you ever thought you
could be. But if you don't want the marriage to work, I have no
psychological or spiritual tricks to patch it up, and God Himself cannot make it work." In about half those cases I find that
the unhappy spouse really doesn't want the marriage to work.

When the person does want it to work, and when the answer is, "Yes, I love this person" or "We love each other but
we're killing each other," I hold out hope. I say, "Listen, there is
an answer for your marriage. We'll find it. Let's pray about it
right now and then talk about it."

"Do you want to be well?" Do you want the love and joy and peace that God offers? Having been given free will, we have the option of saying no. God cannot force His health, His life, His kingdom, His life-style on anyone. It is a choice.

In this life it's never too late to make that right choice, but sometimes we're just too proud to make it. About ten years ago, a friend and neighbor of mine was dying in a nearby hospital. He was an avowed atheist, but his wife was a member of my church. Despite my attempts to convince him to reconsider, the last time I visited him, he said, "Bruce, I know I'm dying. When I do, I may discover that you and my wife are right and I'm wrong. But if there is a God and there is a heaven, I am too honorable to change my mind. If I bet on the wrong thing all my life, I'll stick by my choice."

I have an old friend named Ernie who was for many years the pastor of a church in the heart of Baltimore. One Sunday he preached on that well-known text from Romans 8:28: "For we know that in all things God works for good to those who love Him and who are called according to His purpose." Later, while he stood at the door shaking hands, a man he had not seen before came up, looked him in the eye, and said, "Pastor, do you believe what you were preaching this morning?" Ernie was startled. "I've never been asked that question before," he said. "Let me think about it." But just seconds later, he said, "Yes, yes, I really believe that with all my heart." The very next day Ernie went duck hunting on Chesapeake Bay with some men from his parish. On the way to the duck blind one of his companions tripped. His shotgun went off and blew out Ernie's eyes. He has been blind ever since.

I met him after that accident. He traveled up and down the East Coast to conferences with his Seeing Eye dog. I have never known a man more full of joy and love and faith and optimism than Ernie. On one occasion he told me, "Bruce, my church is in revival. More people are coming, more people are accepting Jesus, and one of the best things is my counseling ministry. I see people who would never come to me if I had sight because they'd be ashamed to be recognized on the street. They can unburden their secret safely with a blind man. My ministry is being blessed because of my blindness."

As a hobby Ernie raised prize-winning dahlias. He always won the blue ribbon at the Baltimore flower show. I don't know how a blind man raises dahlias, producing beautiful blooms he can never see. Beyond that, how does a blind man become so well and whole that he blesses countless people? I don't know. I just know that blindness has not prevented Ernie from finding wellness and wholeness in abundance.

"Do you want to be well?" We've talked here largely about physical wellness, but, in the words of one of my book titles, there's a lot more to health than not being sick. Being well presupposes that we are free from addictions, that we are able to give and receive love, that we are functioning adequately at home and at work, and that we are pursuing healthy relationships. In short, it means being all that God has in mind for us.

If our problem is addiction, there is no better answer than the AA recovery program, which can move us, with God's help, toward wellness. But it can work only if we acknowledge we have a problem and admit we want to be well. With any illness, emotional or physical, healing can begin only when and if we are open to it.

During a research project more than a decade ago, I spent some time with the staff at the Menninger Clinic. One of the questions I asked was if they could pinpoint the single most important ingredient in healing. The answer? Hope—hope that you are not a prisoner of your track record, that you don't have to be what you have always been, that tomorrow is going to be better than today. As medical people they are powerless to instill this attitude. It comes from within.

We could say it comes when, at some level, we believe God has given us a choice. We hear Jesus' question, "Do you want to be well?" and we claim that wellness.

CHAPTER SIX

"Who Do You Say That I Am?"

YEARS AGO WHEN my wife and I first started to date, I couldn't wait to find out what kind of a person she thought I was and what I meant to her. Was I interesting and exciting? Was I a bore and a nerd?

My three children assure me of their love, but in their growing-up years their opinion of me was not always clear. Was I merely their protector and provider? Was I just a soft touch? Did they like me and enjoy me? Did they sometimes make fun of dear old Dad and laugh at me behind my back? Were they ashamed of me?

As for our friends, we can't always assume we know what they think of us. Do they gossip about us and despair of us? Do they stand up for us and admire us? Do they enjoy being with us? Would they go out of their way to help us? Whether or not we dare ask others what they think of us, their perceptions define the kind of relationship we have with them.

If God is someone who wants to have a relationship with His creation—namely us—and is not simply the prime mover, a first cause, a theology, or a creed, then nothing makes more sense than the question His Son Jesus puts to His disciples then and now, "Who do *you* say that I am?"

Three of the gospel writers, Matthew, Mark, and Luke, all record this same exchange. The twelve disciples had been traveling with Jesus for a considerable time. They were present for the Sermon on the Mount and heard His teachings. They had just recently witnessed the feeding of the five thousand. They had been party to His healing ministry and seen the lame walk, the blind receive sight, and the maimed made whole. Now they were being called on to make a judgment about all they had seen and heard. Jesus asked, first of all, "Who do people say that I am?" They told Him that some say He is John the Baptist, others Elijah, and still others Jeremiah or one of the prophets. That's when He posed that second crucial question. "But who do *you* say that I am?" He wanted to know who they, His intimate companions, thought He was.

It is the impetuous Simon Peter who spoke first, and his answer, "You are the Christ, the Son of the living God," is profound. Jesus seemed moved. He told Peter that God Himself had revealed this to Him. Further, he would, from then on, be called Peter (for *rock*), and he would be the rock on which the church would be built. Peter was to become the single-minded and steadfast force behind the early church in Jerusalem.

Names are a shaping force for all of us. Studies indicate that women with fashionable names such as Debbie and Cindy and Jennifer get preferential treatment at school and in the workplace over women named Agnes or Emma or Beatrice. Then there are the names, often derogatory ones, we acquire in childhood that are connected to our attitudes or behavior. When children are repeatedly called stupid, lazy, or clumsy, they tend to fulfill those expectations. There are a number of instances in the Bible where a new name produced a new personality.

Jacob, the patriarch, was a slippery character who managed to deceive his father, cheat his brother, and take advantage of his father-in-law. His name, which literally means "supplanter," or "cheat," was given him at birth because he came from the womb grasping his twin brother's foot, as if to challenge his place as the firstborn. In an encounter with an angel of God at the brook Jabok, Jacob received a new name, Israel. He went on to be the revered father of twelve sons, and those sons headed the twelve tribes on which the Israelite nation was founded.

In the story we're examining, Peter's new name becomes one he eventually lives up to. Over time, the weak and waffling Peter, who denies Christ at the time of His arrest, turns into a new man, stalwart and unwavering. It is through people like Peter—who make the same kind of response to the question, "Who do you say that I am?"—that the church continues to be built.

That same question, "Who do you say that I am?" can be an explosive one in interpersonal relationships as well. In a marriage counseling situation, each person is forced to see his or her self through the eyes of the other. The wife may say, "I know who you are—a bully, a withholder, a miser." The husband responds with his view of her—"a neurotic, a minimizer, dependent, no fun." Then there are the couples who have bought into a different but far from healthy scenario. One feels so lucky to have married the other, and that other party agrees!—"You *are* lucky to have married me." In any successful marriage, each partner thinks he or she is lucky to have found the other and privileged to share that person's life.

That special feeling can last a lifetime and beyond. There's a lovely poem written over a century ago by an English poet, Leigh Hunt.

> Jenny kissed me when we met,
> Jumping from the chair she sat in;
> Time, you thief, who love to get
> Sweets into your list, put that in!
> Say I'm weary, say I'm sad,
> Say that health and wealth have missed me,
> Say I'm growing old, but add,
> Jenny kissed me.

In extreme old age there is a tragic loss of identity for most people. It would take courage to ask, "Who do you say that I am?" The answer might be, "You're someone who doesn't count anymore—whose sight and hearing are fading, whose strength is failing, and whose world is shrinking." Hunt's poem reminds us that this is also someone who experienced love—a love that began with an impetuous kiss and a love that has nurtured and sustained his life.

"Who do you say that I am?" We all, at some point, must answer Jesus' question. Our reply will define our relationship with Him from that point on. If we reply that He is our Lord, He becomes the center, the plumb line by which all we do and are is measured.

Giving up control represents a major revolution for all of us. Not only do I want to control my own life; I am unhappy much of the time because I can't control the people around me. I can't make my parents love me the way I need them to. I can't make my spouse behave in ways that please me. Certainly I can't dictate how friends or employers or anyone else in my life will act or react. I can't control the unfairness of life. I am constantly at the mercy of unpredictable events and the haphazard acts of others.

Our desire to control and be in charge can be the cause of much frustration and anger. Jesus offers us a way out of that trap. Words like *conversion* or *being born again* may put us off, but they simply describe the process of reorienting our lives around a new authority. You are no longer the sun around whom others orbit. God Himself is the center, and we, plus all the people with whom we are in relationship, orbit around Him. That is the radical transformation that takes place when we answer Jesus' question, "Who do you say that I am?" with "You are *my* Lord."

As we said earlier, the disciples were asked first of all what other people thought about Jesus, and some of us wish our dialogue with God could stop there. We can answer that first question easily. "Sir, my mother loved You very much! She brought me to Sunday School and church every week. She read the Bible to me, prayed for me, and told me all about You." All of that is beside the point. We can be thankful for a godly mother or father, but God has no grandchildren.

In the best-selling play *Life with Father*, by Clarence Day, the tyrannical father of a Victorian household full of boys believes in this kind of secondhand faith. He says to his wife, "I'm counting on you, Vinnie, to get me into heaven. God thinks you're special, and He will do whatever you say." Unfortunately, none of us is able to make that transaction for someone else, much as we would like to for a beloved spouse or a straying child. We have to respond to God's question personally.

We may feel we need not answer for ourselves because we belong to an evangelical Bible-believing church. Jesus is preached, and altar calls are extended regularly. But again, the fervor and orthodoxy of some group we may belong to does not relieve us of our own responsibility in dealing with the person of Jesus.

Even our theology cannot be a substitute for the personal response Jesus requires. Jesus tells Martha, who is mourning the death of her brother Lazarus, "I am the Resurrection and the Life. Whoever believes in me will never die." He goes on to ask, "Do you believe this?" But her reply seems evasive. It is like a shortened Apostles' Creed: "I believe you are the Christ, the son of God, He who is coming into the world." Belief in a creed does not liberate us. The devil is a consummate theologian. He understands God completely, how He works and what He does. He knows all truth, but he is still God's enemy.

I avoided that probing question of Jesus', about who He is, for a good many years, and I used all the evasive tactics we've been discussing. I grew up in a Christian home, or at least my mother was a profound Christian. She took me to church faithfully and pressured my father to go as well. She sang hymns all day long, and she prayed for me and witnessed to me tirelessly.

Ours was a staid and Calvinistic congregation, and I can't remember a time in my life when I did not believe in the Apostles' Creed. I've been a believer for as long as I can remember.

But Jesus was some distant religious figure. He was certainly not the Lord of my life.

While still a teenager, I served in the army in World War II. But after the war, as part of the occupying forces, I found myself in a moral meltdown. Anything and anyone was for sale for some nylons or a chocolate bar. I hated the corruption and immorality all around me, but I was part of it. I knew that going home, starting college, beginning a career, getting married would not change me. I'd still be this same weak and sinful person.

I was all alone one night, standing guard in a bombed-out factory in Stuttgart, Germany, when things changed dramatically. I was thinking about my life to date and my inability to be the person I wanted to be. I thought about the God I had always believed in, and I put out my cigarette, took my carbine off my shoulder, knelt down, and began to pray: "Jesus, if you really are there, take over my life. I can't promise you I'll change, because I am weak, but I want you to be the Lord of my life." My life from that moment on took a whole new direction, and, even with occasional detours or mishaps along the way, that direction has never changed.

I'm convinced that our churches are full of unconverted believers just like me. I keep meeting them. A man came to me the other day for counseling. He was in a midlife crisis involving an assortment of problems—a divorce, failing health, a vocational change, and alienation from his children. He said, "Pastor, before you give me any advice I want you to know that I've been raised a Christian by my mother, I am an elder in my church, and I believe in God the Father, Son, and Holy Spirit. I believe in heaven and hell, the cross, and the Resurrection. But what good does all that do me?"

I thought and prayed for a long time and then told him my own story—that I had been a believer all my life and finally met the person I believed in, Jesus Christ. "Have you ever met the person you believe in?" I asked. He asked how he could do that. "One way is to follow some of the first steps of the Alcoholics Anonymous program. Admit that you are powerless to change your life. Believe there is a Higher Power, a person we know to be God in the person of Father, Son, and Holy Spirit. Then turn your life over to that power." He said, "How do you do that?" I said, "Just talk to that person you've always believed in."

He managed to mumble some simple prayer such as "Jesus, I give you my life." As we talked further about that new commitment, he suddenly asked, "Can I pray again?" This time he prayed for about five minutes and included some specific areas where he wanted and needed God's help. Before he left my office, he asked to pray yet a third time. In that last prayer he pulled the cork on his whole life, good and bad, assets and liabilities.

It was the start of a relationship with the living God that is continuing to change that man's life. My new friend had always believed in God, but he had finally been asked to consider the question, "Who do you say that I am?" His enthusiastic answer was and is, "My Lord and my God."

What does it mean practically to make Jesus Lord of your life? It means waking up each morning and saying something like this: "Good morning, Lord, I love you, I'm glad you love me. Thanks for this new day. What is your agenda for today? I want to be a part of it. Show me how I can further your ends through my job and my relationships." We can keep talking to God all day long and wait for His direction and expect it to come.

The timing of this question to the disciples is noteworthy. Jesus did not ask it when He was recruiting those first twelve. The relationship began with a simple request: "Follow me." It's probable no two in that first group had the same reasons for following Him. There are many possibilities. They may have followed out of boredom with their present life or fascination with this new teacher or simply out of curiosity. We don't know. But as the relationship continued, they were called upon to make up their minds about this man. Was He an unusual teacher who had some unexplainable gifts for healing, or was He who He said He was, "the Resurrection and the Life"—in fact, the Messiah? The question had to be answered, and it still does. "Who do you say that I am?"

There are some spiritually attuned people who seem to know and understand who Jesus is from the outset. That was the experience of Helen Keller, that glorious, incandescent saint who was born blind and deaf. When contact was finally made with her through Anne Sullivan's incredible ministry and she was told about Jesus, she responded, "I always knew there was someone like that," and she gave Him her heart immediately.

After a lifetime I've come to believe there are only three ways to live your life. We might call them the three levels of spiritual evolution. We are all born at the first level, the level of feelings. We do what feels good, and we live entirely by our instincts. If it feels good, we do it; if it doesn't, we don't.

As I watch my grandchildren I'm aware that the very young are all at that level. A child simply wants what feels good and resists with tears and tantrums those things that don't feel good. My younger grandchildren will outgrow temper tantrums and learn before long better ways of manipulating people, beginning with their parents. Later on they will learn social graces to manipulate their peers and their teachers and their employers. Society requires a civilized veneer, but at heart any number of people are still living at the instinct or feeling level. They may be unprincipled villains or they may be kind, generous Sunday-school teachers. But their behavior is based on what feels good and what will serve their ends. Just don't get in their way!

But most of us move on to a conscience level. We know there are written and unwritten rules, moral laws such as the Ten Commandments. We begin to live by duty or by the "oughts" of life. This is a major goal of most religions. Religion requires us to shape up and do right and be decent and honest citizens. Certainly it is more mature to live at this conscience level, but it's constricting and often joyless.

What God offers us is a third level of life—a love affair with Himself whereby everything that He has becomes ours and all that we have is His. When we abandon ourselves to that kind of relationship, we have moved beyond feelings or conscience. We don't just do what feels good. We don't just do what we ought to do and what society requires. We go far enough for the fun.

This is what the Christian life offers. A man I know is in the construction business. He builds houses for a living. Just recently he went on a mission with Habitat for Humanity, the group that builds houses for the poor all over the world. It was the most rewarding experience of his life. He didn't need to change his vocation, but he wanted a better reason for building houses. He's moved into that third level we're talking about. He's gone far enough for the fun.

An old friend named Gert Bahannah was converted late in life. Prior to that she was a wealthy, spoiled woman, much married and addicted to both alcohol and pills. She was radically transformed and eventually became a powerful evangelist. But she never stopped being a crusty old character, which was part of her charm.

One day she told a group of us a story that I'll never forget. She traveled by car between speaking engagements and frequently found herself in gas-station restrooms, most of which were filthy. On one such occasion, she was complaining silently to the Lord about the disgraceful condition of the facility. The Lord seemed to say, "I know, Gert. I have to come into these restrooms, too." Struck by that realization, she began to clean up the room—pick towels off the floor, wipe the mirror, wash out the bowl. She left, saying to herself, "Jesus, it's all ready for you now." From then on, she never left a public restroom without cleaning it up for the Lord.

Since then I find myself doing the same thing, mostly on planes or in airports. On that third level of life, we do more than we want to do and more than we ought to do. We move into serving God and doing His will with joy.

Those who began to follow Jesus because they were curious or intrigued or loved adventure or for whatever motive stayed for another reason. They had answered His question, "Who do you say that I am?" with a clear statement of faith. They were called to high adventure. So are we.

CHAPTER SEVEN

"What Is Your Name?"

CHILDREN, WHO ARE habitually asking questions, have always had some unusual ones for God. In the book *Children's Letters to God*, a little girl named Lucy writes, "Are you really invisible or is that just a trick?" Charlene asks, "How did you know you were God?" Jane's question is practical: "In Sunday School they told us what you do. Who does it when you are on vacation?" Dennis's concern is deeply theological: "My Grandpa says you were around when he was a little boy. How far back do you go?"

Our childhood questions are wonderfully inventive, but we are plagued with profound questions all through life. Perhaps the four most fundamental for most of us are: Is there a God? What is His nature? Who am I? What is my purpose in life?

Those four questions seem to sum up a host of other questions we have about life and about God. But if we have met God and begun a relationship with Him, some of those questions have been answered for us. We have come to understand that God's nature is loving. He is our friend. We are beginning to discover our purpose in life—to be His hands and feet and heart to a hurting world as we respond to His call.

But that leaves the third question, "Who am I?" It is a pivotal question and a difficult one. Am I the person I am at work, the person I am at a party, the person I am at home? Jesus focuses on this quest of ours to discover who it is we really are when He asks a very disturbed man this innocent-sounding question: "What is your name?"

Jesus had just climbed out of the boat after crossing the Sea of Galilee. A man came running to meet Him, a man who was called a demoniac. He had been diagnosed by his neighbors as a bona fide mental case. They had tried repeatedly to restrain him, but he kept breaking the chains. An outcast from civilized society, he lived alone in a cemetery. As he saw Jesus approaching he had a brilliant stroke of insight, as demented people sometimes do. He knew immediately who this was. He ran toward Jesus, but his words contradicted his behavior. He said, in effect, "Leave me alone."

Jesus perceived the man's problem and commanded the demons to come out of him. Then He asked pointedly, "What is your name?" "Ah," the man said, "my name is Legion, for we are many." He had so many conflicting identities, he no longer knew who he was. You may remember that Jesus sent this host of demons into a herd of swine and they plummeted off a cliff.

The recorded dialogue between Jesus and that troubled man is all too brief. We don't know what transpired or for how long. We seem to have the *Reader's Digest* version. We know only the nature of Jesus' initial question and the final outcome. The man was liberated from many troubling and conflicting identities.

"What is your name?" is another way of saying, "Who are you?" A true and positive sense of identity is essential to our well-being and our emotional health, but we know that there are any number of people to whom society is sending messages that undermine their feelings of self-worth. During the Los Angeles riots of 1992, newspapers were full of stories of the disturbing events of that crucial time. A man named Marcos Antonio Ramos, a Salvadoran who had immigrated to Los Angeles nine years earlier, was almost killed by six or seven men who tried to kick him to death. When he escaped, he tried to signal the police, who ignored him. He says, "At no time did I see protection from police, even though I asked for it. I made signs to the policemen to come to my aid, but they didn't respond. It was like I didn't exist to them.

"It makes me feel real bad, like we Latinos don't have any rights here, like we're worthless. The police don't see you as a person, as a human. I know I'm a person. I know I'm a person with worth. I have never done wrong to anyone."

One of the most tragic fallouts of civil riots anywhere is that people tend to lose their sense of identity. They get caught up in some kind of mob mentality that negates their humanity. Antonio Ramos, however, did not lose his humanity. He says, "I pray to God that He helps me not to feel resentment over the people who beat me, that I will not accumulate hatred, because we are humans and we err."

If God cares supremely for His creation, then it follows that He desires for each one of us to become everything we were meant to be. Each one of us is a unique, unrepeatable miracle of God. But we get frustrated if we think God is demanding perfection.

That verse, "Be perfect, therefore, as your heavenly Father is perfect" (Matt. 5:48), has been mistranslated over the years to our detriment. The word *teleios*, which has been translated as "perfect," really means "complete" or "all you were meant to be." The implication that we can be morally perfect people is both misleading and an impossibility.

To be complete presupposes having an integrated identity, and that is the goal of all counseling, be it psychiatric, psychological, or pastoral. In a wide variety of disciplines, the goal is to help people achieve an integrated self and to feel good about that self.

Why can it be so difficult to answer Jesus' question? Why are we so confused about who we are? Where do those messages come from that tell us whether or not we're making it, whether or not we have succeeded? What are the forces that shape our ideas about what we should be doing with our lives? I would suggest there are just three sources from which most of us construct our identity: family, society, and our own inner selves.

Let's start with the family. Early on your family begins to shape, both verbally and nonverbally, your sense of worth. But no family is totally healthy, and no family is an entirely positive force in shaping the lives of its members. In some cases, it is a destructive force. For example, your family may have indicated that they think you are a problem person or a loser—not in those words, but in powerful nonverbal signals. Or your family may have communicated that you are a darling who can do no wrong. The world is sure to disabuse you of that idea.

Perhaps your parents were so caught up in their own difficulties from economic pressures, physical or psychological problems, sexual frustrations, or vocational uncertainties that you were mostly neglected or overlooked.

In this day when we speak so much about dysfunctional families it is comforting to realize that every family described in any detail in the Bible is in some sense dysfunctional—starting with Adam and Eve and their two sons, Cain and Abel. The patriarch Abraham had a child out of wedlock with Sara's maid, and that was the cause of enduring enmity. Abraham's grandson, Jacob, conspired with his mother to deceive his father and cheat his brother. Jacob's son Joseph was so hated by his brothers that they sold him into slavery.

At best, families give us mixed messages, and usually, from our teenage years on up, we start looking to another source for our identity—society. Society has many yardsticks, such as how much money we make or have in the bank. We are judged by our vocation, by our looks or lack of looks, by the power that we wield, by our degrees, our wisdom, or our knowledge. Our worth is measured by our fame or by our circle of friends and their status or importance. On a higher plane, society may judge us by our contributions to it.

At any rate, all of these sources of identity are transitory and fleeting. The famous and the rich can be out of favor or broke the next day. Savings-and-loan presidents are now in jail. Even Donald Trump's fortunes have waned. General Noriega, once a wealthy dictator, is in prison for criminal activities. Former movie stars are unemployed and destitute. A millionaire athlete has gone to prison. If we are taking society's measurement of us seriously, we are in for a disappointment.

This is a true story: Years ago there was a Charlie Chaplin look-alike contest at Monte Carlo. Some of Charlie's best friends were there to do the judging. They were unaware that Charlie himself had entered the contest. He ended up in third place! His identity went undetected even by intimate friends.

Teachers have a special role in this business of shaping our identity. For a long time now educators have been aware of something called the Pygmalion effect. It was first described by Harvard psychologist Robert Rosenthal in the mid-sixties. His study illustrated and confirmed clearly that "when teachers are told certain students are gifted or have high potential, whether the students turn out to be gifted or not the teachers look, smile, and nod at them more often. They also teach them more content, set higher goals for them, call on them more, and give them more time to answer. The favored students do better." For many of us, our identity was shaped by teachers who ignored us or by teachers who blessed us with their high expectations.

Even when we are looking only to ourselves to find and understand our identity, we run into problems. It's hard for any of us to have discernment about our own gifts and potential. Within the Christian community, we need each other to perceive and reinforce our best selves. You can perceive gifts and abilities that I didn't know I had. I tend to be either too confident or too humble, but I rarely assess myself accurately.

The demoniac said his name was Legion. That's still our problem much of the time. We have many roles but little sense of true identity. A poem from an unknown author puts it this way:

Within my earthly temple there's a crowd,
There's one of us that's humble, one that's proud,
There's one that's brokenhearted for his sins,
And one that unrepentant sits and grins.
There's one that loves his neighbor as himself,
And one that cares for naught but fame and pelf
    [that's money and possessions],
From much perplexing care I would be free,
If I could once determine which is me!

From time to time in workshops, I ask participants in small groups to tell the other members who they are apart from family status, job, or any titles they may possess. Most people are baffled by this request. We're so used to defining ourselves by whether we are married or single, by our job as a teacher or mechanic or salesman, or by our education and training and degrees. Think about it. You are more than your family, more than your job, more than any titles that society has given you. Should you suddenly lose your family and your job and move to a primitive society where titles were of no value, you would still be you. How do we describe that you—that core that is independent of all those touchstones?

For seventy years the Soviet Union told its people there was no God. God was replaced by the state, and the state defined the identity of its citizens. If the government is faltering and failing and cannot function, the self-worth of its citizens is undermined. Only the hopes and dreams that emanate from a sense of self-worth can produce a state that will benefit and bless its citizens.

When the Communists dismissed God as an antiquated notion, they also rejected the whole concept of sin. They believed in the perfectibility of man, a concept that is biblical heresy. Christians believe we are a fallen people who, without God, do not act in the best interests of others. Unredeemed, we all act out of self-interest. We don't have false expectations that a new system will make people perfect. Our whole Western enterprise of government and commerce is based on that same biblical view of man. "Who are you?" is an important question even in the game of world politics.

The demoniac's encounter with Jesus effected a dramatic change. The people from the village came out, perhaps some hours later, to find a man who had been healed of his mental illness. Mark, in his Gospel, describes the man's new state and includes three signs of wellness that are indications of an integrated identity, then and now. First, this former madman is sitting at the feet of Jesus, which means that he is under authority. He is no longer a law unto himself. Second, he is clothed. He has a sense of morality, an understanding of what is decent and what is right and wrong. Finally, the text says he is in his right mind. He sees himself accurately, and he perceives life around him as it really is.

Those continue to be important marks of emotional and mental well-being. We are moving toward a healthy sense of identity when we understand, first of all, that we are not the center of the universe, when we can submit to authority when it is appropriate, which means accepting correction or guidance without hostility. Crucial to emotional health is an active conscience that keeps us from using and abusing other people. But the third quality that the demoniac demonstrates is perhaps the most essential. A positive sense of identity gives us a handle on reality. We don't maximize or minimize ourselves or our problems. We don't overdramatize our situation but are able to evaluate it with clear judgment.

The demoniac was transformed as a result of his dialogue with Jesus, a dialogue that began with a question that went to the heart of the problem. "What is your name?" God is still in the business of giving us new names and new identities. The Bible provides many Old and New Testament examples for us. We mentioned Jacob, for whom a new name meant a whole new personhood, and Simon, the big vacillating fisherman who was renamed Peter and whose new name meant "rock," which was what Peter proved to be throughout the early years of Christendom. Saul became the apostle Paul, and another early Christian named Joseph was renamed Barnabas, which means "son of encouragement," and that's what he was. It was Barnabas who smoothed the way for Paul's acceptance by the church at Jerusalem, and he was that kind of "bridge person" in every situation, according to the book of Acts.

It is only as we enter into a relationship with God that we begin to have an understanding of who we are. The prophet Zephaniah writes, "The Lord your God is with you, He will take great delight in you, He will quiet you with His love, He will rejoice over you with singing" (Zeph. 3:17). It is a wonderful image—that God is singing over us because He so delights in us. Sometimes I wake in the middle of the night and envision that that is happening. It is a source of great comfort.

In the time that I have served as co-pastor of the Crystal Cathedral, I have been very impressed with the consistent and unique message that Robert Schuller has communicated for almost forty years. He wants people to know that they are important. The breathtakingly beautiful Crystal Cathedral was designed to communicate that message. The building itself says, "You are important." It is a gorgeous structure, made of glass, fit for royalty, and that's what the gospel tells us we are. But a lot of churches out there are propagating a different message. Worshipers are told they are worms and miserable sinners. Of course we are all sinners! But we can be redeemed sinners who have found the love of God and the joy of serving Him.

A verse from Proverbs reads, "Do not withhold good from those who deserve it, when it is in your power to act." That's the ministry of affirmation that I have been preaching all my life. People need to hear they're doing a great job. They need to be affirmed, encouraged, and reminded of how much God loves them.

One of my favorite books is *Don Quixote*, by Cervantes. The hero, a senile old man, sees people not as they are but as they might be. Before the book ends they have become the people he envisioned. We have that power—to see others as God sees them.

I discovered that even the clergy sometimes need to learn to do that. An Episcopal priest who was my friend and neighbor underwent a great transformation during the years I knew him. This somewhat uninspired and uninspiring clergyman became a man on fire, and his church caught that fire. Of course, I wanted to know what had happened to him. He said, "Bruce, it happened on a retreat with some of the other priests from our diocese. The bishop was there serving Communion, and I went to the rail to receive it along with the other priests. As he served me, he said, 'Tim, this is the body of Christ broken for you.' I was stunned. I didn't know the bishop even knew my name. I began to see myself differently from that moment on."

That's hard to explain, but I believe Tim came to realize that God knew his name simply because the bishop did. Freedom and power began for Tim with that affirming encounter. He felt encouraged. He felt loved. He felt important.

Those of us who are married often fall into the trap of seeing ourselves only as our mates or our families see us. That happened to a woman I know. She and her husband were our good friends. Her health failed, and she required a number of operations, which took a great physical toll. She was no longer the lovely young woman her husband had married. He became distant and cold. She responded with truculence and faultfinding. Eventually, he left her for someone else.

Fortunately, she attended a small group all during this time, where she could share her sad story. The members prayed for her and loved her. In time she no longer saw herself as a neglected and abused wife. That minifamily of God helped her discover that she was a beloved child of God. She went back to school, got a job, reestablished herself, and is now a positive, radiant Christian. She has a new name. She is no longer a victimized wife, a discarded lover. She claims the name that God always had for her.

I have always loved the Old Testament story of Joseph because of the many times he was able to handle and overcome so many tragic and unfair circumstances. Joseph was one of twelve brothers. He was the favorite of his father because he was the firstborn of Rachel, his father's favorite wife. When the brothers were given new clothes, only Joseph got a striped coat. It was as if the eleven brothers were given bib overalls from JC Penny and Joseph got a silk smoking jacket. Of course the other boys hated Joseph. If that were not enough, he boasted to his family about his dreams—dreams in which all the brothers were bowing down before him. They were angry enough to want to kill him, but they decided instead to sell him into slavery. But while they were deciding exactly what to do with him, they put him down a well.

I've always wanted to preach on that part of the story and call it "Thoughts down a Well." What do you think Joseph thought about while he was down there at the mercy of his brothers, with his fate hanging in the balance? He had at least three options. He could blame his family for his predicament— his father for so patently giving him preferential treatment and his brothers for their merciless revenge. He could blame himself; how foolish he was to brag and incur all this hatred. Or he could say, "I am your person, God. Whatever they have done or whatever I have done, I know you love me and you mean it for good." As we read the rest of the story, of course God did mean it for good. Joseph becomes the second most powerful man in

Egypt and is eventually in a position to save the whole family from starvation.

Have you ever felt like you're down a well, sometimes a well of your own making? That's the perfect time to find God's new name for you. "What is your name?" That's Jesus' question to the demoniac, and it's His question to us. God is in the new-name business. He wants us to know that even at our worst, He sings over us in the night and rejoices over us by day.

CHAPTER EIGHT

"What Do You Want Me to Do for You?"

MY WIFE READ something a while back that she enjoyed enough to quote on every possible occasion: "Sure, Fred Astaire was a great dancer, but let's not forget—Ginger Rogers did everything he did, backwards and in high heels."

In the last few decades, women are finally being heard, and old wrongs are beginning to be addressed. The women's movement has impacted all of our lives. And recently some authors have been addressing the problems of men. Robert Bly has received a lot of attention for his book *Iron John*. He uses myth, fairy tales, and images from Carl Jung to explore the passage to manhood in America.

Sam Keen, author of *Fire in the Belly*, says, "Sensitive men have finally, after 25 years, begun to hear what the women's movement is all about." Keen calls it a "gender revolution." The underlying theme for some of these books seems to be, "It's our turn." It's not surprising that, with the changing roles of men and women and the resulting confusion about who we're expected to be, books titled *What Do Men Really Want?* and *What Do Women Want?* are being snapped up not just in bookstores but at the supermarket.

In this present climate, the question we're considering now seems strangely contemporary. God is asking men and women of this or any culture or time, "What do you want me to do for you?" That is the question Jesus asked a blind man, according to Mark's Gospel. He and His disciples were leaving Jericho, and a crowd had formed to see them off. In the crowd was a blind man named Bartimaeus, which simply means son of Timaeus. As he heard the crowd noises increase he sensed that Jesus must be getting closer, and he stood up and shouted out, "Jesus, Son of David, have mercy on me!"

The people around him rebuked him, I'm sure, with phrases like "Be still!"; "Shut up!"; "Who do you think you are?" But he cried out even louder. Jesus heard him and called out to him to come forward. Bartimaeus groped his way through the crowd toward the sound of Jesus' voice. Jesus then asked him that probing question: "What do you want me to do for you?" The man said, "Rabbi, I want to receive my sight." The man was healed there on the spot and joined the group following Jesus.

Oddly enough, Jesus asks that identical question earlier in the same tenth chapter of Mark. James and John have come to Him with an open-ended request—that they be granted whatever they ask for. Jesus, with those same words, replies, "What do you want me to do for you?" He must have been disappointed with their answer. They wanted special favors in heaven, more privileged positions than the other ten disciples would have.

However, Jesus did not appear to know how James and John would respond to His question or what it was they wanted of Him, even though they had been His intimate traveling companions and friends. Just as with the stranger named Bartimaeus, the request had to be voiced. Jesus did not assume He knew what they wanted. They were free to ask whatever they wanted.

The question has important implications. God is not like some doting grandfather or lady bountiful who presents us with the goodies that *He* wants to give us. He asks what it is we want. Our answer is a barometer of our own value system. How would we reply? We could say we want a new BMW or that we want to become famous. We could ask for a cure for our mother's cancer or our child's illness. We may want to win the lottery and never have to work again.

I wonder if the blind man had any regrets in later years about his request. We don't know what happened to him, but let's construct a possible scene some ten years down the road. Let's suppose, as he reflected on that encounter with Jesus, that he said to himself, "I stood in the presence of the very Son of God and I asked for my sight and got it. Since then I have been able to see, and it's wonderful, and I am grateful. But there were so many areas of my life that needed healing. I have married several times in these intervening years, and each time my spouse left me. My parents have given up on me, and I rarely see them. I can't seem to hold a job because I don't work well with other people. My life is full of hatred and bitterness and broken relationships. I don't even like myself. What might I have asked for from Jesus that could have changed the way my life has turned out?"

Certainly Bartimaeus wouldn't have minimized the gift of sight, and neither do I. Every morning I wake up and thank

God I can see. I have glaucoma in both eyes, and it's possible I will be blind before I die. But as much as I thank God for the gift of sight while it lasts, I suspect there are gifts He would give me that are far more important than even my sight.

God is able to cure our diseases, but His primary aim for His children involves an eternal cure—the cure of souls. Our soul is our uniqueness, our personality, our very identity. We could say it is our value system. It is the part of us that will live forever. The body, including our eyes, will cease to exist, but we believe as Christians that the soul lives forever and that each one is unique.

Scientists tell us that the electrons and protons and neutrons that make up the atoms of the body are mostly space. That means we are scarcely more than a walking, breathing thought from God. The physical is minimal and temporary. The spiritual remains intact and lasts forever.

We have all been fascinated by the old Faustian legend with its emphasis on the importance of the soul. The devil makes a bargain with Faust: "If you give me your soul I'll give you whatever you want in this life." Of course, Faust chooses wine and women, fame and fortune, not realizing that what he has lost has supreme value and that the devil will be the one to profit by the bargain.

A Man for All Seasons is a drama that remains a favorite of mine. It is the story of Sir Thomas More, who has angered the king because of his attitude toward a royal divorce. He does not publicly disapprove, but he has too much integrity to give his blessing to the king's plans. His careful attempt to walk some middle ground ends when he is brought to trial for treason, betrayed by an old friend whom he helped some years earlier. In return for false testimony, the cardinal has appointed More's old friend to be exchequer of Wales. As this betrayer is about to leave the courtroom, having told lies that will send Sir Thomas to his death, More looks up at him and says, "The Bible speaks about exchanging one's soul for the whole world. But for Wales?" The scene prompts all of us to examine our own ambitions. Is there something important enough to trade your soul for?

One of the Old Testament's most famous stories is the one in which Esau sells his birthright, the blessing and inheritance of the firstborn, to his brother Jacob for a mess of pottage, which is a sort of stew made with game. He had been out in the field and is so famished that everything else is unimportant. He wants instant gratification. That's often the framework in which we are tempted to sell our souls. We want something, and we want it now—sexual gratification, wealth, fame, success, or political power.

I recently read about a young man named Stan Vetock who decided, at age twenty-nine, to stop trading his soul for luxury living. He was a successful realtor making $130,000 a year and enjoying all the good things of life—a five-bedroom home, a string of luxury cars, expensive clothes, and posh restaurants. In October 1989 his priorities changed. He decided to fulfill his dream and go to college, maybe even play football.

He ended up in Auburn, Alabama, where he supports himself by delivering pizzas and cutting grass. He hadn't played football since the seventh grade, but he made the team. He's far from a star, having spent the whole first season on the bench and playing only occasionally and for short periods since. His ex-employer says this about Stan: "He could have made a fortune working for me. . . . He chose not to come back. . . . We all thought Stan was a little crazy but at the same time we understood. . . . Stan had other priorities."

Stan Vetock's value system had undergone a radical transformation. Jesus' question, "What do you want me to do for you?" forces us all to examine our value system.

While I was on retreat a few years back with a small group of men, we zeroed in on this question: "What is it that you fear more than death?"—or "What is the worst thing that could possibly happen to you?" There were seven men present, and there were seven very different answers. I said that my greatest fear was to lose my first love, which is Jesus Christ, and to die bitter and unbelieving, denying Him. I have watched this happen to a few close friends who had been devoted Christians and charismatic leaders.

In a letter to Timothy, Paul speaks about Demas, who, "in love with this present world, has deserted me" (2 Tim. 4:10). I can't imagine anything worse than losing my lifelong faith in a God who loves me. But, as you can imagine, many fears were mentioned—incapacitating illness, the loss of a spouse, the death of a child. But as we discussed our deep-seated fears, we were in a position to more truthfully answer God's question, "What do you want me to do for you?"

When we use this question to understand our own value system, we find that all of life's choices are simplified. Even making a purchase such as a house requires an understanding of our priorities. When my wife and I moved from Seattle to southern California we went looking for a place to live. We looked at dozens and dozens of houses, but none of them matched our list of priorities. At the top of our list was location—proximity to my new church. Two, I wanted a view. We had spent ten years looking out at Lake Washington, and we were spoiled. Three, not being a Mr. Fixit, I was holding out for a newer house. Four, I like a house with lots of sunshine, with big windows and few trees. Well, we finally had to decide between a new house and a view house. We ended up buying an old house with a view, and in spite of many costly repairs, we love it more every day.

But a house purchase is just one area that requires an understanding of your priorities. Each new job, new friendship, new opportunity to serve somewhere in the church or in the community forces us to examine our priorities.

If you were face to face with Jesus, as Bartimaeus was, how would you answer His question? Would you ask for the gift of faith so that you would never again have to wonder in good times or bad about the existence of a God and the reality of His love for you? Would you ask for the gift of love so that you could weather whatever comes—indifference, rejection, hostility—knowing you are forgiven and able to forgive those who hurt you? Would you ask for the gift of joy? I know people who have that gift in abundance, even when life has dealt them unfair or tragic blows.

One of my heroes is an old friend who died in a nursing home, a frightful one, smelly and dark and overcrowded. She had lost her husband, her children had abandoned her, she had no money, and in her last years she lost her sight. But every visit with her was an "up." On Saturday afternoons Mrs. Thompson gathered other members of the home around the little radio in her room to hear the broadcast of the Metropolitan Opera, explaining the plots and commenting on the singers. She was a tireless witness for Jesus in that sad place. God had given her the gift of joy, which was like a beach ball: it could not stay submerged for long, whatever life's circumstances.

Would you ask for the gift of courage so that you'd never be afraid again and would be able to do whatever was required? The following poem by Edna St. Vincent Millay celebrates the courage God had given her mother.

The courage that my mother had
Went with her, and is with her still;
Rock from New England quarried;
Now granite in a granite hill.
The golden brooch my mother wore
She left behind for me to wear;
I have no thing I treasure more;
Yet, it is something I could spare.
Oh, if instead she'd left me
The thing she took into the grave—
That courage like a rock, which she
Has no more need of, and I have.

Would you ask for the gift of creativity? That gift is present to some degree in all of us simply because we are made in the image of God. We are the only animals we know of that can create ex nihilo even as God does. We are like Him in that one respect. We can write poetry, build bridges, invent lifesaving machines, start movements.

There is no one in my experience who is more creative than Ken Medema, the songwriter, musician, performer, and evangelist. He can take a crowd of several thousand and turn them instantly into a close, intimate group. He performs after a sermon or speech or witness, composing, on the spot, a song that goes to the heart of what has just been said. Ken Medema was born blind. I don't know if there's a connection between his blindness and his extraordinary sensitivity. Who and what would Ken be had he not been born blind? If God were to ask him what he wants most now, would it be his sight? He has already surpassed most of us, without his sight, in his creative abilities and his effectiveness.

Many of the gifts we've been listing here are the fruits of the Spirit that God offers to us. The question is, What do we want Him to do for us?

Asked by God what he wanted, King Solomon asked for wisdom, and he got it. He wrote the book of Proverbs and was considered the wisest man of his time. A few years ago that might have been the gift I wanted most. I have always aspired to be wise in the ways of people—their motives, their behavior, their dreams. In my later years I have changed my mind. Wisdom, as valuable as it is, is not what changes the way we live. Some of the wisest people I know are unhappy and unfulfilled and are contributing little to the rest of society. On the other hand, I know people who do not profess to have much wisdom but who seem to have learned the secret of a loving and joyful life.

So many of the gifts we've mentioned turn out to be gifts for others as well. The old sampler rhyme says, "The love in your heart wasn't put there to stay. Love is not love till you give it away." The same is true of our faith and our joy, of our courage and creativity and wisdom. Those are not qualities that can remain bottled up. They are bound to spill over to bless and enrich the lives of others.

Ernest Hemingway was a man of monumental talent, but when we read about the way he lived and his death by suicide, we don't think of him as a man of wisdom. Yet he did have at least one very wise practice. On the first day of each new year Hemingway gave away some of his most prized possessions. People invariably asked why, and his answer was always the same: "If I can give these things away, then I own them. But if I can't give them away because they have somehow become so important to me, then they own me." That's a wise way to live your life. As I said earlier, we are meant to love people and use things, but in our consumer society we often end up loving things and using people.

I think we all need to be bolder about asking for what we want. Oliver Wendell Holmes, the famous jurist, once wrote:

A few can touch the magic string,
And noisy fame is proud to win them;
Alas for those that never sing,
But die with all their music in them!

Dying with all our music still unsung is not God's best plan for any of us. He wants to help us be everything we can be, *everything* He had in mind for us from the beginning. We can start by telling Jesus exactly what it is we want Him to do for us and acting on the conviction that He can and will do it.

CHAPTER NINE

"Who Is My Mother and Who Are My Brothers?"

WE'RE HEARING A LOT these days about family values, about the importance of the family—meaning the traditional two-parent household with one or more offspring. But for a significant segment of the population, this is not reality and there is no way that kind of ideal unit can, by some magic, be brought into being. Those single parents are forced to work with the situation as it is and to wrest from it something positive for their children.

Those very people may find comfort in a question Jesus asked in regard to family and in His remarks about the nature of His family. While Jesus was teaching a crowd, He was told that His mother and His brothers were outside the room asking to speak to Him. He turned to His disciples, and the rest of His hearers, and asked an unusual question: "Who is my mother and who are my brothers?" Then, pointing to the twelve who had risked everything to follow Him, He announced, "Here are my mother and my brothers. For whoever does the will of my Father in heaven is my brother and my sister and mother."

That is the vision Jesus had for His followers then and for all those who would follow down through the centuries. His words indicate that He wants us to be a family, His family. At supper with His disciples on the final night before His trial and crucifixion, He prays: "My prayer is not for them alone [i.e., the disciples]. I pray also for those who will believe in me through their message, that all of them may be one, Father, just as you are in me and I in you. May they also be in us so that the world may believe that you have sent me."

Jesus must have startled his hearers. The Jews, then and now, place great importance on family. What a revolutionary idea it is that, whatever our existing family, single parent or no parent, no siblings or unrewarding siblings, a positive force or a negative one, there is another family we can be a part of— God's own family. This is central to Jesus' dream for His disciples in this or any age.

Perhaps the greatest failure of the church in our day is that so much of our time and energy goes into buildings and programs and we ignore Jesus' dream for who we are to be to and for one another.

We in the church get distracted by so many other concerns and priorities. For years I traveled from coast to coast speaking or conducting conferences in various churches. I was struck by the fact that most churches have a unique profile in terms of message or mission.

Some stress authentic worship. Records of New Testament times are searched in order to duplicate first-century liturgy and music. Some emphasize stewardship. Tithing is expected. The budget is balanced. There must be no indebtedness. For a good many churches, a strong, biblically literate preacher is the main attraction. In others, the focus is on evangelism or missions or outreach to the community. There are "signs and wonders" churches, and there are those that major in spiritual healing.

All these emphases are good and admirable, but there is no greater priority than being the family of God to each other. That is the base on which all our ministry needs to be built—evangelism, education, outreach, giving, and authentic worship.

Jesus' question, "Who is my mother and who are my brothers?" strikes a chord in all of us. Families are pervasive and powerful shaping forces. It is within families that most of us develop our self-awareness and our self-esteem (or lack of it). Families have the power to enhance or damage our spiritual, social, mental, and emotional life.

Family reunions are always popular, sometimes drawing relatives in the hundreds who gather from far-flung places. My guess is that not all of them are entirely happy affairs, but most people would not miss this chance to reassemble with their clan or bunch. Though we did not choose them, these are the people whose genes and history are inextricably bound with ours. These are the people who give us identity, true or false. They call forth our gifts or repress them. They can be a source of encouragement or can inhibit and constrict us.

My parents were both Swedish immigrants who met and married in Chicago. My mother was forty when I was born, my father was sixty, and I'm an only child. I had no sisters or brothers, uncles, aunts, cousins, or grandparents who could help me over difficulties and encourage me in my life's journey.

About ten years ago my wife and I went to Sweden and met my mother's relatives for the first time. They are gracious, wonderful people. Mother was the oldest of twelve children, so there were many, many uncles and aunts and cousins to welcome us with open arms. Some months later, after our return home, we received a photo in the mail. It was a picture of the annual family reunion. That big crowd of relatives had gathered out in a lovely meadow in summertime Sweden and were sitting around a table groaning with good food. In the center, they had placed an empty chair, signifying my place at the family table. That was the message on the back of the photo. I had finally found my bunch.

My wife and I have three children—a daughter, who is the oldest, and two sons. One of our fondest family memories is a six-week car trip we took one summer. We started in New Jersey and traveled all the way down the East Coast into Mexico, then up the West Coast, and back to New Jersey by a northern route. We did all this in an un-air-conditioned Volkswagen bus that we had purchased especially for the trip, and we brought along Duke, our forty-pound springer spaniel. The very first night out we camped, and Duke relieved himself in the tent. He spent the whole trip sitting on the ice chest in a catatonic state that continued for months after we got home. I think he suffered a canine nervous breakdown. On another memorable night, camping on the Gulf Coast, we were attacked by swarms of blackflies.

The kids spent all their traveling time with their heads buried in Donald Duck comic books while I yelled things like "Listen, kids, this is the Grand Canyon. Look at it, for Pete's sake!" We got stuck crossing the Mojave Desert behind a truck carrying two dead cows to a rendering plant. Our little van lacked the power to pass, and with no air-conditioning, all the windows had to be open. The stench was unbearable. Later in the trip, we arrived at a friend's home in Portland, Oregon, to find Duke missing. It dawned on us that we'd left him 150 miles back at a gas station. But my most vivid memory is driving mile after mile in our sluggish van over incredibly boring terrain, while simultaneously reaching into the backseat trying to punch any one of my three kids, yelling, "Will you stop that fighting!"

Guess what? Today the five of us remember that as a truly wonderful trip. As I tried to figure out why, it occurred to me that for six brief weeks we were a family, interdependent. We needed each other to simply survive. We were a working unit, and we learned some new relational skills.

"Who is my mother and who are my brothers?" With this question Jesus points out that true families are not only biological families. This fall I attended my first army reunion. I fought with the 100th Infantry Division in World War II. The members of my platoon of Company I, 397th Infantry Regiment, have been getting together now for several years. They reminisce about the wonderful times we had during the war. Mostly, they were terrible times of mayhem and bloodshed. But we were family. We cared for each other, we fought together, we depended on each other. We were there for each other. We watched our comrades die. For some, life may never again have seemed so meaningful.

A while back I was speaking at a renewal conference attended by pastors and church leaders from many churches all over the city. After I spoke, I divided the crowd into groups of four and gave them some simple questions to answer such as "Who was in your family of origin?"; "What kind of communication took place around the dinner table at night?"; "When did God first get your attention?"; "What is your dream for the next two years of your life?"

I joined one of the groups, and we shared for about an hour. Afterward an elderly man turned to the rest of us and said, "I have been a member of my Presbyterian church for fifty years. I have taught the senior-high class there for forty. I have been an elder and a deacon for thirty. What's more, I spend almost three evenings a week at the church with church activities and meetings." At that point he looked at the three of us with tears in his eyes and said, "In just one hour I've come to know the three of you better than I know anyone in my church!" Apparently, in all those years in his own church community he had not found those mothers and brothers in the faith that Jesus spoke of.

The notion of family today seems under a cloud. People who come for counseling often tell me that their real problems began with their dysfunctional family. "Who is my mother and who are my brothers?" We all seek an ideal family, but as I pointed out earlier, to some degree every family is dysfunctional.

Let's look at Jesus' own family. Scholars assume that Joseph died early on and that Jesus' mother became a single parent with four sons and an undetermined number of daughters. We don't know exactly why His mother brought all her other sons to the meeting where Jesus was speaking, or what her motive was in asking that He come out. Did she intend to rebuke Him? Was she going to criticize His methods or His timing? Mary is surely one of the bravest women in biblical history, but she may not have been the kind of mother Jesus needed at this point in His ministry.

The story of the prodigal son and the elder brother paints a picture of a somewhat dysfunctional family. The son who is a reckless profligate is resented by his dutiful, hardworking brother. The elder brother accuses the father of having favorites. Part of the Good News in the Bible is that we are all bad and that families, even at their best, are to some extent dysfunctional.

Most of us have two families. We have our family of origin, the family in which we grew up, and then we have a family of choice. That second family is made up of our spouse and our offspring, if we have any, and it includes our intimate circle of friends. Our family of origin may produce in us a determination not to marry someone like Mom or Dad. But once married, it isn't too long before we find ourselves saying, "My gosh, you are just like my mother!" We find the dysfunction of our family of origin being repeated in our family of choice. I should say here that in no way do I mean to make light of genuine and severe dysfunction where abuse is taking place, be it sexual, physical, or emotional. I'm saying rather that every family is, to some extent, flawed.

One of the most poignant stories I know is told by Brooks Adams, one of our gifted writers. His father was Charles Francis Adams, who was for years our ambassador to England and a very busy man. On one occasion, the father and son spent the day fishing, and Brooks, who kept a diary, as most men did in those days, recorded the event as one of the greatest days of his life. He had his beloved father all to himself out in the woods for one whole day. Years later, when his father died, Brooks inherited all his father's records, including his diaries. Eagerly, he searched for his father's entry for that special day. The inscription was devastating: "Spent the day fishing with my son. A day wasted."

If, as I'm saying, both the family of origin and the family of choice are either mildly or severely dysfunctional, then the thrust of Jesus' question is especially relevant. "Who is my mother and who are my brothers?" Those people who, with me, call God Father and make up His family. The only enduring hope for a healthy, life-giving, esteem-building family is the family of God. He loves us. He sees our need for a family. His dream is that His church, the family of God, will fill that need. That's what Jesus was telling His disciples and what He continues to tell us, His present-day disciples. We are to be mothers and fathers, brothers and sisters to each other in liberating ways that our family of origin and family of choice have failed to be.

Within the community of faith, some of you can become the mother I never had, giving the affirmation she couldn't give, yelling, "Atta boy, Bruce, you're great, go get 'em." And some of you can become the dad who died when I was eighteen while I was serving in the army. As old as I am, I still need a dad to be a role model. And some of you can be my siblings, those sisters and brothers I longed for as an only child. And conversely, I can be a dad and a brother to others in this family of faith. This is Jesus' dream for His church.

When Jesus asked, "Who is my mother and who are my brothers?" He indicated that the disciples were filling that role. They had become a family. Jesus said, "Follow me!" to twelve busy, working men, and with that call came enforced intimacy with each other. Each one was plunged into a shared life with eleven other men. They traveled together, they ate together, they failed together, and they succeeded together. Jesus urged them over and over again, "Love one another as I have loved you."

Intimacy was not optional for those first twelve, and it is not optional for us. This is why small groups are so important. In these groups we become family, and we have the power to bless and release and heal one another as we travel together on this amazing journey of faith.

When Jesus raised Lazarus, His beloved friend, from the dead, He instructed those standing around to "loose him and let him go." That's our job as the community of faith—to unbind each other. We can't raise the dead; only Jesus can do that. For Him there are no hopeless cases. But if and when those hopeless cases begin to find new life, we are called on to unbind them that they might experience their full potential.

There is a conspiracy against intimacy in the church today. Sharing our lives in small groups—our day-to-day failures and victories—is threatening and scary. A few years ago, a fellow pastor told a group of us that he had never had a parishioner to his house for dinner, nor had he been to any of theirs. We were astonished, and he went on to explain, "Well, I learned that in seminary. They said we are professionals. When you become intimate with your congregation you undermine that professional

relationship. I've followed that advice." His church is diminish-
ing, incidentally, and it's not surprising. He has missed one of
the important functions of the church, which is to be a family
not only eating together, but supporting each other in sorrow
or joy.

Most of our Christian education programs are not designed
to promote intimacy. Sunday by Sunday we focus on teaching a
curriculum, forgetting that the people who come to those
classes, children as well as adults, have tremendous burdens
and pressing agendas in their private lives. In addition to content, there ought to be opportunities to reach out to each other
personally—to bear one another's burdens, to be those mothers and fathers, brothers and sisters Jesus spoke of.

When I started my ministry in Seattle I realized early on
that the opportunities and demands of that big parish were
going to be overwhelming. On my first Church Officers' retreat, I said to the thirty-six elders that I needed help. Would a
few of them promise to meet with me for an hour and a half a
week and hold me accountable and pray for me? Six men vol-
unteered, and for the next ten years the seven of us met together at seven o'clock every Friday morning to pray for each
other, to encourage each other, and to read the Bible. We never
talked church business. We focused on our own lives and how
to become the people that God wanted us to be.

More recently, I came to the Crystal Cathedral in response
to an invitation from my old friend and brother Robert
Schuller to join him as a co-pastor. I said I would come on the
condition that he and I meet regularly to share and pray. Since
then Juan Carlos Ortiz, preacher for the Spanish "Hour of

Power," has joined us, and that small group has been a powerful source of blessing to all three of us.

Has your family of origin failed you? Has your family of choice disappointed you? There is hope. Jesus says of His family, "*These* are my mothers and my brothers [and my fathers and my sisters]." Join them.

CHAPTER TEN

"Why Are You So Afraid?"

THROUGHOUT THE Old and New Testaments, our heavenly Father gives us some surprising advice that has nothing to do with obedience or morality, at least not directly. The admonition, repeated often, is "Fear not" or "Don't be afraid."

This was needed advice in biblical times, and it's needed advice now. Fear is perhaps our oldest and deadliest enemy. Fear causes illness. Fear kills. Fear stifles creativity. Fear prevents love, disrupts families, and can lead to all sorts of addictions. None of us is free of fear at all levels.

But there is a vital link between fear and faith for every Christian. Jesus made that point on an occasion when He and His disciples were confronting a very dangerous situation—a storm at sea. He had spent the day teaching the multitudes. Exhausted and ready to escape the crowds, He told His disciples to get in the boat and start across the Sea of Galilee. Almost immediately, Jesus fell asleep in the stern.

Meantime a violent storm had come up, which was not unusual on the Sea of Galilee, ringed as it is by mountains and subject to fluky winds. Some of the disciples were seasoned sailors, but even they found the storm terrifying. The boat was taking on water and was in danger of sinking. Jesus, who had slept through all this turbulence, was forcibly awakened by the disciples. "Master, don't you care if we perish?" they asked. Jesus woke up, took in the situation, and rebuked the wind. Calm was restored. That's when He asked the question we're considering here: "Why are you so afraid?"

You might say the question seems odd. Who would not be afraid in a small boat that is in grave danger of sinking at night in the middle of the sea? Fear would be a very normal reaction. The apostles had never been promised a life of safety and security, and that is not promised to us. God's own Son, Jesus Himself, was not protected from harm. He went through a terrible ordeal beginning with His trial and ending with those painful hours on the cross. The remaining apostles all eventually died martyr's deaths. They neither expected nor sought a life of safety and security.

But Jesus followed His question with another: "Do you still have no faith?" Faith requires trust—that whatever happens, our lives are in God's hands. I love the Old Testament story of Shadrach, Meshach, and Abednego, the three young men in exile who were threatened with death in a fiery furnace because they would not worship other gods. In a brave speech they told the king that their God would deliver them and that even if they were not delivered, they would still worship the one God and trust Him. They were immovable.

I had a phone call a few months ago from a former parishioner who has a history of heart problems. Her doctor had warned her that death could be imminent, and she was in the grip of overwhelming fear. After much conversation, I finally asked, "Winnie, are you prepared to die?" After a pause, she said, "Yes, I am. I've loved Jesus all my life, and He has promised me eternal life." "Then let me ask you a second question. Are you prepared to live on God's terms—perhaps with impairment or diminished capacities?" I had put my finger on her real fears. She wasn't ready to trust God with that bleak possibility.

That is surely the sense of Jesus' second question, "Do you still have no faith?" Deliverance from the storm was incidental. The disciples were not yet at the place where they trusted Jesus with their future, and at the moment they were caught up in the obvious dangers of their situation, and they were afraid. We identify with their feelings.

Fear is a part of all of our lives from childhood on. It is impossible to live life without it, and perhaps it was meant to be so. Fear can provide the handle by which we take hold of God Himself and learn the basic rudiments of faith. Let's examine some of the fears that are common to all of us.

There are healthy fears. These are the kind of fears we need in order to survive. Children are taught to fear hot stoves and sharp knives and matches. They are taught to fear busy streets and strangers who offer them rides. In adulthood healthy fears may keep us from smoking or using drugs. The fear of AIDS can lead to more responsible sexual behavior. The list goes on. It would be stupid not to fear things that endanger our health and well-being.

But many fears are neurotic and can lead to psychological impairment. One of these is called free-floating anxiety; it's a constant nagging state of uneasiness about things we can't even name. Neurotic fears take many forms, and most of us are familiar with terms such as *paranoia*, *claustrophobia*, and *acrophobia* (fear of heights). Some neurotic fears are extreme and require treatment from professional therapists and trained counselors.

Then there are the normal everyday garden-variety fears. Let's face it: life presents us with fearful situations at every level—from childhood to old age. There is an element of fear in every new challenge—starting school, changing jobs, getting married.

In answer to Jesus' question, "Why are you afraid?" most of us would mention some fears that seem primal or basic. One is the fear that we will be unable to control or handle our lives. We have already said that the first temptation was to want to be like God—to be in control and have power over ourselves and others.

Until my recent surgery, I thought that I had reached a level of Christian maturity where this was not a problem for me— that I had placed my life and destiny in God's hands. But as I said earlier, I had never been in a hospital before, and I found that the prospect made me fearful. I had a hard time making the decision to go ahead with the surgery.

I don't think I was afraid of death. I have been getting ready for death most of my life and expect to welcome it when my time comes. I was somewhat afraid of impairment. Would I survive as a whole person after the surgery? How radically different would my life be? Would surgery affect my sex life? My wife reminded me that I've been preaching to single people for years that life is more than sex and now I had a chance to test that philosophy.

But above and beyond any of those fears was the fear of falling into the hands of the medical establishment. During and following the operation, I would be at the mercy of strangers. An anesthesiologist would hold my life in his or her hands. A surgeon would be slicing my stomach open. Unknown nurses and doctors would have to get me through the crucial days of intensive care. I found I was terrified to be in that powerless position. And that fear is, I think, basic. That's why we are so fearful of illness and old age. We will no longer be autonomous, but at someone else's mercy.

Perhaps an even more primal fear is the fear of abandonment. That fear starts early on, probably in the crib, where we howl for food or a dry diaper, uncertain if anyone will ever appear to meet our needs. Those fears are present throughout our early years as we're left in the care of baby-sitters or a kindergarten teacher. Will our loved ones ever come back? Have they abandoned us forever? I think it's the fear that Jesus speaks to with His question to the disciples in the sinking boat. Did they think He had abandoned them or that He would?

Never having seen God, we all wonder at times if He is really there and, if He is, whether He is our friend and will hear us when we call upon Him. Even Jesus faced that fear in the Garden of Gethsemane just before His crucifixion. He cried out, "Father, let this cup pass from me." His later words on the cross underscore that greatest of all fears. "My God, my God, why have you forsaken me?" God had not forsaken Him, but

Jesus, tempted in every way as we are, felt forsaken. He feared He had been abandoned.

Fear is a given: healthy fears, neurotic fears, everyday-type fears, and primal fears. Robert Schuller, in his book *Life's Not Fair, but God Is Good*, reminds us that all of us live in a world that is unfair, where bad things do happen to good people. But in the midst of those trying times there is a God who wants to be our friend and who offers us help and hope in every situation.

The last book I wrote is titled *Living Beyond Our Fears: Discovering Life When You're Scared to Death*. In it I discuss how we can handle some of life's basic fears, including the fear of failure, of death, of rejection, and of the past.

The only sure way to deal with fears and to overcome particular fears is to stop avoiding them. A psychiatrist I know treats a number of patients who fear leaving their homes. He encourages them and even accompanies them as they start making small excursions—first just a few steps from the house, then to the end of the block and farther. With each day's victory, there is a gradual subsiding of this irrational fear. That approach, of hitting our fears head-on, is an important tenet of Gestalt therapy. The theory is that the avoidance of pain and fear destroys life. The alcohol and pills we take to overcome those emotions become more of a problem than the pain and fear. I learned that lesson in a secular setting, but as I read my Bible the idea was reinforced. Jesus, on the cross, refused the drugs that were offered Him to ease the pain.

"Why are you so afraid?" We are urged to explore that question. Some of us are victims of paralyzing fear, the kind that makes us a prisoner of our own psyches, our own homes, or our own narrow worlds. Seeing a counselor can help us get to the root of such extreme fears. More commonplace fears often manifest themselves in a lack of risk taking. We fear meeting new people or new challenges, or we dare not put ourselves in a situation where we might fail. These kinds of fears need to be shared with other Christian friends, ideally in some support group that meets regularly. Those are the fears God wants to and can help you with as you pray about them, as you, with His help, begin to take steps to overcome them.

Our lives are shaped by the way in which we handle life's difficulties, including our fears. A favorite poem seems to speak to that point as no other. It's by Ella Wheeler Wilcox.

One ship drives east and another drives west
With the selfsame winds that blow.
'Tis the set of the sails
And not the gales
Which tells us the way to go.
Like the winds of the sea are the ways of fate,
As we voyage along through life;
'Tis the set of a soul
That decides its goal,
And not the calm or the strife.

Someone has said that too many people are waiting for their ship to come in who never sent one out. It seems to be a rule of life that cautious living produces little in the way of rewards and dividends. It's the bold and risky ventures that have the possibility of stunning success. It may mean launching out into a new job, a whole new vocation, leaving the secure and the comfortable. Jesus asked His disciples, "Why are you so afraid?" and He is asking us that same question. He was with them, and He has promised to be with us.

We all play ball in the rain; we all live in an unfair world. From cradle to grave we are subjected to frightening experiences. But the direction of our lives determines whether those experiences will strengthen or destroy us. If our lives are based on faith in a God who loves us and who offers to be our friend, we can face our fears with courage and conquer them. The Bible says perfect love, which is God's love, casts out fear.

I heard about a circus performer, an animal trainer whose act involved putting a number of tigers through their paces. One night, to the horror of the audience, all the lights in the circus arena went out just as this man stepped into the tiger cage. He panicked for a moment but soon began speaking to the tigers and cracking his whip in the usual manner. Nobody could see what was actually happening in that cage, but the crowd was terrified.

Before long the lights came back on, and the act continued normally. Later someone asked the trainer what it was like to be in a cage full of tigers in the dark. "At first I was very frightened," he replied. "I knew the tigers could still see me, for they can see in the dark. Then I realized that those tigers had no idea I wasn't able to see them. That's when I began to speak and crack my whip as I always do. It worked because they were utterly unaware of any change in the usual procedure."

There's a faith parallel in that story. Jesus rebuked the disciples with His question, "Do you still have no faith?" Faith requires acting as if God were in control of the situation, which in fact He is. When the lights go out and we don't feel safe, that's the time to act as if God is present and still working in our lives.

In 1990 I moved from Seattle, the land of mighty firs and oaks, to southern California, the land of palm trees. In both locations I learned some new things about trees. I'm told that cutting off a belt of bark a foot or so wide around most trees will kill those trees because only the outside bark is alive. Palm trees, on the other hand, have a living center and tough, scarred outer surfaces. They have a simple external structure with few branches and few air-catching leaves. In strong winds they bend, sometimes touching the ground, but they won't break. When the wind dies, they straighten up again.

Palm trees have an unusually strong root system that extends deep into the ground and therefore can find water in arid places. Palm trees are able to survive drought. While most trees eventually get too old to bear fruit, palm trees don't even begin to do so until they are fifty years old. What's more, it is the oldest palm trees with the scarred trunks that bear the sweetest fruit.

That's a wonderful insight into the Christian life at its best. Our life comes from the inside, flowing from our relationship with God. We are not to be encumbered by too many material possessions. They will only hinder us when the strong winds of life start to blow. Our roots go deep into our relationship with

God, and our fruits—the fruits of the Spirit—are even more in evidence as we grow older.

There's a good deal of poetry written about the mighty oak, but in weathering the storms of life the scruffy palm tree has the advantage. Like it, we may look frail and vulnerable and for too long unpromising in the fruit-bearing department, but we are able to survive the storm.

The disciples, on that frightening night in their wind-tossed boat, survived the storm. Jesus calmed the waves immediately. Nevertheless, He did not prevent the storm from occurring, which He might have done. We Christians, like those early followers, are not guaranteed any safe place. We have only the promise that He will be with us "even to the end of the age." Fear not.

Afterword:
The Other Side of Prayer

FINDING GOD is the single most important and transforming experience of life and one that has been shared by men and women of every description for thousands of years. The problem is to find fresh language with which to describe that life-changing encounter. It has been called, among other things, conversion, being born again, making a commitment, being saved, or coming home. But the experience itself transcends all barriers of age or circumstance.

It can happen to the very young, and it can happen to an old person on his or her deathbed. It happens to people born to privilege as well as to those raised in poverty or with abusive or insensitive parents. It can happen to orphans, to the homeless, to the drunk, and to the dope addict. It can happen to successful executives on top of the heap, with honors piled high and all the money they need.

For people of any age, at the bottom or the top, this sudden or gradual awareness comes: there is a God who made everything we see, who made us. He knows our name, knows who we are. And He says, "I love you! There's a purpose for your life now and forever. Let me show it to you." That is the moment of awareness—the curtains part, the light bulb goes on, the relationship begins.

What prompts this awakening we're talking about? For the prodigal son it was his unpleasant circumstances. He had squandered his inheritance. He had lost his friends. He had been reduced to taking a job feeding pigs and not eating as well as they were. His motivation to return home was purely selfish. But his father came running to greet him. He didn't say, "You made your bed, now lie in it." He said, "My son, welcome home."

That same awakening happened first to Abraham and Sarah, a prosperous couple living in Ur of the Chaldes. These Old Testament heroes had a pioneer faith in a God who called them into an obedient relationship. Unlike the prodigal, they had nothing to gain materially. They understood that there was some higher being who had a plan for their lives and for the whole human race. They sold all that they had, rounded up some camels and donkeys, and started off along with their nephew Lot and his family. They began a journey of unknown duration to an unknown destination. The only property Abraham ever owned again was his wife's burial plot. It seems crazy, doesn't it? But a life-changing experience took place to prompt all that.

The New Testament gives us the story of Nathaniel, who had a similar awakening. Jesus saw him approaching and said, "Look! An Israelite in whom there is no guile." Apparently that was rare. Most of us are full of guile, not just the Israelites. Jesus discerned that Nathaniel was a rare one, a man without guile—a transparent man. Nathaniel was flabbergasted. They had never met, and yet Jesus knew him. He knew his strengths and not just his sins. He discerned something in Nathaniel that perhaps nobody else had seen. The awakening can come simply because God reveals your strengths to you, strengths that have been overlooked. Surely, it was a similar awakening that made all twelve disciples leave their families, their businesses, and their jobs and follow Jesus. They were betting their lives and their futures on Him.

I met the Lord as an infantry sergeant in Stuttgart, Germany, during World War II. In the first months after I returned home I vividly remember walking the streets around my church in Chicago. It was located on the edge of the tenderloin and surrounded by some of the seamiest neighborhoods in the city. As I walked those streets I had the feeling that I'd discovered a great secret about God and His love for me. I felt sometimes like a deep-sea diver, with an air hose connecting me to light and grace. Nothing could stifle my joy, nothing could overwhelm me, because I had a pipeline to the source of life. I wanted to shout at the defeated and dejected people on the street, "Listen! You can have an air hose, too. You can be connected to a God who loves you, and you can transcend this terrible, depressing environment." You could say I had a new awareness.

Having awakened to God's love, we are constrained to express our love to Him in some tangible way. I was struck by that recently on a trip to Austria and Hungary. I had an unusual opportunity to look at some of the different ways people over the centuries have responded to God's love.

As any trip to Europe will confirm, one common response was to build a building—a big and beautiful cathedral. If we truly love God He must have the finest building in the city. Whole generations gave their money and their skills to the erection of these magnificent places of worship. Europe, and even America to some degree, is dotted with great buildings put up by the labor and the sacrifice of people responding to God's love and His claim on their lives.

Others have, over the centuries, expressed their love by renouncing the world and all its pleasures. Life is so full of enjoyable pleasures—a warm and comfortable home, a good night's sleep, a hot shower, coffee in the morning, and friends and loving families. Some have felt that in order to show one's love for God, all that must be given up. We must live out in some desolate place, wear simple homespun clothes, and eat soup or oatmeal three times a day. Sleep is interrupted several times every night to sing and chant and pray. Any number of sincere Christians over the ages have expressed their love of God in that way.

We have to admire these monastic Christians. For them, God is more to be desired than the best the world can offer. I'm sure God, who reads the heart, honors their motives. John the Baptist was the New Testament model for this Spartan lifestyle. He wore animal skins and ate grasshoppers. Further, he had some doubts that Jesus was truly the Messiah because He went to parties and seemed to enjoy life.

Other groups have responded to God's love with study and scholarship. They devote their lives to mastering theology. They spend their years poring over sacred writings and early manuscripts. Theology, of course, is the science of God. But if God is a personality, as I've stated earlier, He is more than a subject to be studied. But for those who have pursued Christian theology for two thousand years, the good news is that God reads their heart and their intent and loves them for their sincere desire to understand Him.

Another way men and women have responded to God over the years is by trying to master the mysteries of God. Those engaged in that effort are the liturgical specialists, caught up in the esoterics of incense, candles, proper chants, authentic music, and all the trappings of worship. They are and have been the stewards of the liturgical traditions, and as such we honor them.

History also points to a fifth common response—the use of military might and power to extend God's kingdom. There are many examples of this. By the fourth century the Christians had turned the Roman Empire into the Holy Roman Empire. In Charlemagne's reign, Christian baptism was forced on conquered armies. The crusaders mounted their holy wars. Men of the time and even their young children were caught up in the idea that they could prove their love for God by reconquering the land where Jesus was born and lived. Over hundreds of years tens of thousands of Christians and Muslims were killed in the effort. Even Columbus's voyage to the New World was an attempt to extend the rule of God's physical kingdom, the Holy Roman Empire.

Finally, we can respond to God's love by pursuing righteousness. To become the righteous person God requires, one must abstain from all that is bad or sinful. There must be no dishonest behavior and no impure thought. But righteousness is not what you don't do, it's what you do. If righteousness were the absence of evil, then the most righteous person in your town would be some patient in the local hospital, comatose, being fed intravenously, incapable of doing or saying or thinking anything bad. God abhors sin, but we cannot make the avoidance of it the primary purpose of our lives. Certainly we esteem those people who try to live scrupulously moral lives, but they are living by law and not by grace.

I spent some time last year in Lancaster County, Pennsylvania, where an Amish community lives. In the name of God and righteousness they refrain from all things worldly. Buttons are considered secular, so they use hooks and eyes. Instead of automobiles they drive horses and buggies. The Amish are pious, hardworking, good people, but their whole focus is on avoiding the worldly contemporary culture around them.

These are some of the ways, past and present, in which we have, over the last two thousand years, responded to God. When we discover a God who loves us so recklessly, so passionately, so unreservedly, and at such a cost we know that some response is required. Even on the human level, a declaration of love requires some kind of an answer. The enlightenment, the awakening, occurs as we hear God saying, "I made you. I've got plans for you. You are forgiven for all of your sins, past, present, and future." As Paul writes to the Esphesians, "You're no longer strangers and sojourners. You are fellow citizens with the saints and members of the household of God."

God reads our hearts, and I think He blesses any and all genuine responses, even some that seem to us misguided. But what response most pleases Him? Jesus sums it up when He says that the greatest commandment is to love the Lord your God with all your heart, soul, mind, and strength and to love your neighbor as yourself. The prophet Micah said, "What does the Lord require of you but to do justly, to love mercy, and to walk humbly with your God." We can't walk humbly with our God by simply attending His church once a week for an hour. If we have had an experience of God and committed ourselves to Him, then a relationship of love begins. He wants to be our friend, and He wants us to love people around us the way He loves us.

I have spoken and written often about the importance of a relationship with God. But what are the ingredients of a good relationship, a healthy relationship—say, with your spouse, your parents, your children, your best friend? Any relationship of quality has the same ingredients. Trust is one of them. You can count on that person. She is there for you, and you're there for her. If my wife and I are separated for a period of time, I want to be able to count on her faithfulness. She wants to count on me sexually, emotionally, financially, and any other way. In a good relationship I can trust that other person with my money, my virtue, my reputation. As we begin that relationship with God, we can trust Him with our lives, our vocation, our finances, even our sexual needs.

Total acceptance is essential to a good relationship. If I totally accept you and you totally accept me, we can level with each other. We can ask for help when it hurts, and we can own up to our shabby behavior. Our vulnerability is met with unconditional love. In the same way, we can open our hearts to God and tell Him how we feel—angry, hurt, disappointed, whatever. He knows anyway, but it's important to practice that kind of openness and vulnerability in any authentic relationship with Him.

A good relationship thrives on affirmation. A withholder cannot be a satisfying lover or a rewarding friend. In any relationship, especially one with family members, or close colleagues and friends, it's essential to say often and whenever it's appropriate, "You're wonderful. That was terrific." No matter how famous or important we are, we still need affirmation. We practice affirmation for God by means of praise. "God dwells in the praises of His people" (Ps. 22:3). He wants us to praise Him—to cultivate an attitude of thanksgiving.

Any meaningful relationship presupposes that you enjoy each other. A relationship thrives in proportion to how much any two people enjoy each other. The Bible tells us that God delights in us. He enjoys us. I am always struck by the first question in the old Presbyterian catechism: "What is the chief end of man?" The answer? "To glorify God and enjoy Him forever." That's even more important than serving Him.

Finally, a good relationship requires the dimension we have been addressing throughout these chapters—two-way communication. You can't have a relationship without listening and speaking—in other words, dialogue. Over the last dozen years, I have counseled a number of couples whose marriages were breaking up after twenty years or more. In my recent experience there are more women leaving their husbands than men leaving their wives. Invariably, the woman has found someone else. I always ask what this new person offers that the present spouse doesn't have. The attraction, it seems, is minimally sexual. What I hear most is, "He listens to me. I am important to him. My ideas are important to him."

Henry Kissinger once said that power is the ultimate aphrodisiac. I think he's wrong. Listening is the ultimate aphrodisiac. A good relationship depends on dialogue, one in which we take the other person and his or her needs and interests seriously. Prayer is not just giving God a laundry list of requests. It's listening to Him and trying to discern His will for our lives.

As we have suggested throughout these pages, on the other side of prayer, God wants to know certain things about you. Perhaps the questions we have considered can provide a starting place. He has many more than I have addressed here, but the ones I have chosen are some of the crucial ones on which our faith hinges and which can lead to a reexamination of our own relationship with our Creator and our Friend.

Let me give you some ways in which you can apply these questions we've examined and make them a means of transforming your life. First of all, you can use them in your personal prayer life. I hope you have a time at the beginning or end of the day that you set aside for God and prayer. That doesn't mean you can't pray while driving down the freeway or riding on a commuter subway. You can pray all day long and without ceasing, and that's what He wants.

But in those quieter prayer times, let God ask you some of the questions we've explored. I suggest you keep a notepad and pencil handy and be prepared to jot down those things that come to mind that seem to be of God.

Where are you? Where are you in your spiritual search right now? Where have you been hiding in the past? How were you encouraged to stop doing so? You might consider writing the details of that experience and using it as a resource for sharing your faith with someone else. It's not enough to proclaim, "I'm a Christian, and you should be one." We need to intrigue others with before-and-after stories like the ones that are used to such advantage at any Alcoholics Anonymous meeting.

Where is your brother? Keep your mind open to some unexpected answers. God may bring people to mind that you have not considered before who need a phone call, a check, a helping hand, a letter, a listening ear.

What is that in your hand? Take an inventory of your resources. What special gifts do you have? What life experiences have you had that God can use? List your personality assets, your financial resources, your network of friends.

Who will go for us? Does God have a specific job for you? Ask Him. List some areas in which you might be able to be His messenger and speak for Him.

Do you want to be well? Ask God to help you explore the unhealed areas of your life—physical, emotional, spiritual, or relational.

Who do you say that I am? This can help you think through your whole concept of God—what you began with as a child and all the experiences and influences that have shaped your present understanding of Him.

What is your name? Make that one a means of understanding your self-concept. Do you like who you are and what you are?

What do you want me to do for you? This can be a wonderful means of crystallizing your priorities and your future goals.

Who is my mother and who are my brothers? Let that question help you reexamine your relationship with and feelings about your family of origin. Beyond that, are there some Christian friends in your life right now to whom you could reach out to fill that role?

Why are you so afraid? Make a list of your conscious fears. God can help you understand them and overcome them.

These questions can, of course, provide the framework for a ten-week sermon series, if you're a pastor, or a ten-week Sunday-school class. They could also be the basis for a small-group study. But however or wherever you use them, I urge you to start dealing with these questions God has asked and continues to ask. I'm convinced the process will be a means of strengthening and encouraging your relationship with Him.

I have often been referred to as the Father of relational theology, and I accept that title even though all sorts of excesses have been associated with the term over the years. I still think, however, that our Christian orthodoxy is measured most of all by the quality of our relationship with God and with other people. A vertical relationship with God is reflected in our horizontal relationship with those around us. Jesus has said, "Inasmuch as you have done it unto one of the least of these, you have done it unto me." He seems to make very little distinction between what we do for Him and what we do for one another—who we are with Him and who we are with one another.

Relationship requires two-way dialogue, and that has been the theme throughout these pages. It is my hope that these questions God asks—on the other side of prayer—are going to stimulate, strengthen, and deepen your own relationship with Him. That relationship is bound to spill over into every area of your life as you put your faith to work across the street or across the world.